MW01167115

ALWAYS, ONLY
GOOD

A journey of faith through
MENTAL ILLNESS

SHELLY GARLOCK HAMILTON

Author's Note

I am not, nor pretend to be, a medical or psychiatric authority on mental illness. My expertise instead is a result of fifteen years spent in 24/7 experience as a mental health caregiver, in-depth reading and research on the subject, and advice given to Ron and me from multiple authorities in the fields of both psychiatry and medicine. I have also had the privilege of spending hours in communication with countless family members of the many who unfortunately deal with the often-misunderstood issue of mental illness. I have seen mental illness at its worst and God at His best.

One thing I have come firmly to believe is that quoting the phrase "God is good" should not be done flippantly when horrible things or joyous things happen. The goodness of God is instead a profound conviction we understand deep within our souls, no matter what happens—both good and bad.

Shelly Garlock Hamilton

Contents

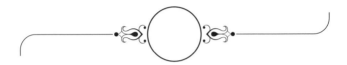

The *Why* Behind the *Words*

As journaled on:

December 9, 2013

The family is a gift from God.

The family unit was designed from above by the divine Creator. Each of its members is fearfully and wonderfully made to be enriched with a sense of belonging—far greater than each solitary life. Sometimes the reality, unfortunately, is far from the ideal, but the fact still remains that the family was created to be a place of comfort, safety, and security.

Family members share many things. Some of the most outstanding physically shared traits are bloodlines and genes. A gene is a unit of heredity that is transferred from parent to offspring. By God's plan, genes predetermine many things about us and our families.

God is awesome.

Whether you believe that our incredible universe happened by chance or that it had an intelligent Creator, you have to acknowledge that something more significant than the human intellect keeps the earth orbiting around the sun. Only by supernatural means do our hearts beat and the fingers of our hands move independently. As a complex smartwatch cannot evolve from an explosion or invent itself over time, I do not believe that an even more complex human body, specifically the brain, could have happened by chance.

This book is not a debate about the existence of God. Important to understand, however, is that I and my family believe in an all-loving and all-powerful God. Seven months have passed since we lost our beloved firstborn son Jonathan, a brave individual who dealt with mental illness. Our story is one that describes a God who remains faithful to us despite of and because of our challenges.

God is the initiator of life, not of sickness and death. Satan gets that credit. By tempting Adam and Eve to sin, he has become the author of bad things. Satan wants us to believe bad things happen because God is not good, but it is instead because Satan himself is evil. If we can solidify the significance of God's love and goodness, we can better deal with all that happens to us—both the good and bad.

January 2017

Four long years pass after our son Jonathan's death before I am able to pick up my pen and write chapter one. I can continue no further. Jonathan's illness and therefore the writing of this book was certainly not my choice. Yet God. Yet God has dropped it in my lap. He will give me the strength I need in His time.

February 28, 2018

Now—in 2018—I gain more courage and am able to complete chapters two and three.

You see, our oldest son Jonathan lived with mental illness for almost fifteen years. My determination to write his story has been great. But at the same time, it is difficult for me to dredge up and relive the emotional pain. I have needed strength and guidance from God above to finish this task.

Finally, in 2020, I feel compelled to continue and hopefully complete Jonathan's story. What a year this has been for all of us. Because of being in lockdown due to the COVID-19 pandemic, I have had more time to write. We will see how far I get this time. My computer keypad is already tear-stained as I have re-read and edited chapters one, two, and three. My grief is now a familiar companion, even though five heart-wrenching years have gone by.

My greatest motivation for writing Jonathan's story is the deep love I have for my son. I also desire to portray that hope runs deeper than despair. Other reasons include:

- helping remove the stigma of mental illness by letting the outsider in.

- helping counselors know better how to come alongside.

- encouraging onlookers to be more supportive.

- encouraging those who live with mental illness to keep taking their medications.

- giving hope to those who live with mental illness and to those who are its caregivers—you are not alone.

- finally, and most important, showing how I discovered God is always, only good—even through mental illness.

September 25, 2020

After receiving a Facebook message last night, I am more determined than ever to share the importance of understanding mental illness.

The message was sent privately from a grieving pastor's wife, Brenda Bickford from Lee, Maine. Heidi, Brenda's 27-year-old daughter, began suffering from depression during her teen years. Now that Heidi was married and had a family, she believed that the older of her two sons, two-and-a-half-year-old Enoch, was demonstrating some of the same depression symptoms.

One evening, Heidi took off in her car with Enoch. She parked by the side of a highway, got out, and wrapped her small son up in her coat. While holding him, she jumped in front of a tractor trailer speeding down the road. She was killed instantly.

The impact of the truck sent her baby boy flying out of her arms. As he landed on the side of the road, a car was passing by with two medical workers—truly a God thing that they were immediately on the scene. Although he had two broken legs and bleeding on the brain, they were able to save the life of precious little Enoch.

Upon hearing this story, I grieve alongside my new friend. Her agonizing account sent a bolt-of-lightning through me. How could I overlook such an important mission to help stop each *Jonathan* and *Heidi* out there before hopelessness took their lives?

Before Jonathan passed, I was invited to speak to a group of ladies. I asked Jonathan if he minded if I shared his story. He replied, "Not if you think it will encourage anyone and as long as you tell them how well I'm doing now." Well, both are still true today. I believe God is urging me to finish his book. It's time!

This is Jonathan's story.

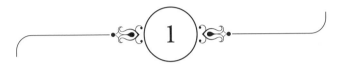

Our Lives Change

6:30 a.m., May 12, 2013

The day begins as a relatively typical Sunday. Although today is Mother's Day, it is a Mother's Day like no other. The Hamiltons are up and getting ready, anticipating the day of worship at Calvary Baptist Church in Simpsonville, South Carolina. My husband Ron is the music pastor, and I play the piano. We have served together in music ministry our entire married life.

All of our kids participate in this ministry with us, including our oldest, Jonathan. Jon, as we sometimes affectionately call him, used to sing solos, participate in the choir, play his trombone, his guitar, and arrange for special music groups. This, however, is no longer the case.

This Mother's Day our son Jonathan is still in bed as we leave for the music audio checks that typically start about 8:10 a.m. For almost fifteen years now, Jonathan has been living with a mental illness condition and rarely goes to church or any other social gathering for that matter. He survives and functions on three different hard-core medications that cause him to sleep at least twelve to fifteen hours a night. Even during his waking hours, he often remains tired.

On Sundays, when he rises early enough to come to the morning service, he has multiple times showered, dressed for church, driven the twenty-five minutes to the property, and then been unable to make himself go inside. Anxiety and paranoia accompany him wherever he goes. He sits in the parking lot for a short while before deciding to turn around and drive back home.

12:30 p.m.

Church on this particular Mother's Day is now over. Ron and I are making the drive back home. Jonathan loves to cook. He has planned and prepared a delicious Mother's Day lunch for me and his two grandmothers—Flora Jean Garlock and Leota Hamilton.

To the best of our collective memory, when we arrive home, we are presented with roasted turkey, dressing, mashed potatoes and gravy, as well as a broccoli, cauliflower, and carrot vegetable medley. Jonathan tops the meal off with homemade strawberry shortcake. (I really don't recall the entire lunch menu but am very certain of the strawberry shortcake, because I find the leftovers several months later in the extra refrigerator in the garage.)

Our family has such a wonderful time of fellowship at lunch. Jonathan is not hungry, so does not sit down to eat. He laughs and jokes as he serves us and then cleans up following the meal. While the rest of us sit around and talk, Jonathan goes into our music library to play some of the beautiful songs he has written.

About 3:00 in the afternoon, all our guests leave. Ron works on preparing for the upcoming 4:45 choir rehearsal. I go into my office to read a grievous letter written to my dad by a family member—not an immediate one—that leaves me devastated and crying.

Midstream into the letter, Jonathan comes and stands in the doorway of my office, speaking with me for about fifteen minutes. Important to mention here are the continual delusional thoughts that circle through Jon's mind—thoughts he has learned to accept as the constant foes that they are.

Although one of his meds is an antidepressant, his depression remains only an arm's length away. Today he begins recounting to me all the reasons why he will never take his life, one of which is his uncertainty that he will actually go to heaven due to his depression, delusions, and paranoia.

These philosophical topics have come up from time to time during his illness. Jonathan has trusted Christ as his Savior, lived a life of dedication to God, and exhibited the fruit of the Spirit the Word tells us about. I assure him he has done what God requires to be His child.

To be clear, I don't under normal circumstances recommend convincing someone else of their salvation. In Jonathan's case, his doubts of salvation and thoughts of suicide have surfaced often enough that I realize he needs to talk through these recurring obsessions, which usually occur when he's off his meds. Ron and I have found that what is required is reassurance that his delusions are not affecting his salvation.

We are sensitively aware of the possibility that Jon might attempt suicide since he has taken the first steps of doing so on four different occasions—each time when he was psychotic from taking himself off his medicines. Fifteen years we have lived with this dark prospect. Deep down inside, however, we believe it will never actually come to pass. I myself refuse to. The mere mention of it is too horrible to dwell on.

While despondent from the letter I am reading in my office, I try to concentrate on what is to be the last conversation any of us will have with our Jonathan. It is difficult to wrap my brain around both Jonathan and the letter.

I remember in this exchange being acutely conscious that Jonathan is again not thinking clearly. His thoughts are going round and round in circles. I recall feeling that maybe I should stay home from church with him. I missed church the previous Sunday due to illness, so I felt that if at all possible, I should go fulfill my responsibility as pianist.

Most evenings are tough for Jonathan. To help him keep any degree of sanity, he usually takes off in his car and drives around for several hours. At times, we go with him, but he prefers to be alone. Even if I had stayed home from church, it is likely he would have taken off in his car without me.

4:15 p.m.

Ron and I leave for the 4:45 church choir rehearsal, which seems to go like normal.

5:20 p.m.

Nearing the end of choir, Ron receives a text from Jonathan but does not read it because he is still directing the rehearsal.

5:55 p.m.

As Ron is preparing to begin the evening service with congregational worship, he reads the 5:20 text from our son. He quickly finds someone to take over leading the music at the end of the service. He arranges for another pianist to take my place. Ron directs the first few songs. As we sit down for the preaching, Ron whispers to me that we need to head home immediately.

As we leave the church, Ron shows me Jonathan's text. After getting into the car, I call our daughter Alyssa to see if she is home. Alyssa is not, so I direct her to get there immediately and look for Jonathan. Next I call 911 and ask someone to head to our address immediately. A detective calls me several times during this trip to ask me questions. It is a very anxious, long ride home.

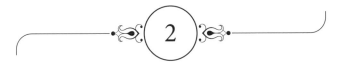

Alice Mae Garlock

The 1930s and 1940s

We will now be stepping back in time to share some family history on the side of Jonathan's grandfather, my father, Frank Garlock, better known as Pop-Pop by his grandchildren. As you read this chapter, the relevance of Jonathan's genetic heritage will become clear.

Alice Mae Garlock, Jonathan's great-grandmother, was one of the sweetest ladies you would ever want to meet. Grandma Alice, as we all called her, was a homemaker and a gifted pianist. She gave birth to nine healthy children—seven boys and two girls. Growing up, every time I went to visit, Grandma Alice gave me a beautiful hanky. I have a large, framed art piece of nine of them. Our close family friend and longtime Patch audio engineer, Gary Emory, calls it my "snot-rag collection."

Jonathan's great-grandfather, Edward Arthur Garlock, flew planes, trained fighter pilots, and was a genius machinist at Casey Jones Aviation Center during World War II. After that, for a brief time, he pastored a small church. He then became an automobile mechanic for the rest of his life. My dad says Grandpa could fix anything.

The Garlock clan was larger than life. Eating at their dinner table was quite the experience. You were engulfed in boisterous laughter and continuous talking which crescendoed louder and louder so each could be heard above the other. I loved the electricity and excitement in the air.

The oldest son, Ed, was in the Marine Corps band during World War II. His unit was responsible for picking up all the deceased bodies after the attack on Iwo Jima. The term PTSD (post-traumatic stress disorder) did not exist until 1980.

During World War I, the term "shell shock" was used. During World War II, the terminology changed to "war neurosis." Ed returned home from the war experiencing extreme physical reactions to loud noises and also waking up with nightmares. In his later years, he developed bipolar disorder, probably triggered by PTSD.

Eunice, next in line, had what was labeled a "nervous breakdown" when she was twenty-four years old. Because Grandma Alice had so much to do with taking care of nine children, Eunice became "mother" to the younger ones. The load of responsibility she carried at such a young age probably contributed to her breakdown.

She developed extreme anxiety and paranoia, went through multiple shock treatments, and was eventually diagnosed with paranoid schizophrenia. After years of experimenting, the doctors were finally able to find a medicine that allowed her to function the rest of her life to the mature age of eighty-seven.

Bob, third in line, formed a musical group along with Ed and Frank during their growing-up years. They traveled extensively as the *Garlock Harmony Trio*. Bob became a sheriff in the Los Angeles police department. One day, when he was returning to his car after serving a woman a speeding ticket, she intentionally backed into him.

Uncle Bob was thrown under the car, which actually saved him from being run over. Her vicious act led to many extensive back surgeries and chronic pain for the rest of his life. His dreams and studying to be an opera singer consequently never materialized.

Frank, the fourth sibling and Jon's Pop-Pop, has been a proficient musician. He started a sacred music publishing company in 1965, now called Majesty Music. Much of his life he has operated on minimal sleep yet still worked endlessly and at full capacity. Frank wakes up feeling very low. But once getting up and going—watch out! He has had what is called eidetic memory, remembering details about what he reads and about his life experiences.

Don, the fifth child, has been creative theatrically. He has taught speech and directed plays on the college level. Don eventually moved to Lynchburg, Virginia, to teach speech, English, and communication at Liberty University. Don, as an excellent speaker, became chaplain for the Liberty University Athletic Teams as well as for the Lynchburg Hillcats Baseball Club.

Elmer, sixth in line, suffered from serious depression and self-medicated with alcohol. Many mental illness sufferers drown their pain with drinking. They feel better while intoxicated, but when the effects of the alcohol wear off, the depression is worse than before. Thus, they crave more and more, eventually becoming alcoholics. Uncle Elmer ironically had been a medic and pharmacist in the Air Force, so he knew the dangers of alcohol well. Because of his excess consumption, he died in his late forties from pancreatitis.

Alice was number seven. She had a beautiful contralto voice and became an opera singer. She also painted beautiful landscapes. Alice, like Elmer, experienced depression most of her life but was able to function well on antidepressants. Aunt Alice eventually died from brain cancer when seventy-three years old.

David was child number eight and a concert pianist. David suffered with episodes of bipolar as a teenager. He had nights when he couldn't sleep and thus practiced the piano instead, disturbing the entire household. These sleepless nights turned into days of inability to get out of bed. Due to diligence and talent, Uncle David traveled as a concert pianist. He unfortunately became addicted to drugs and took his life with an overdose while on a concert tour in California. He was just twenty-eight years old. The week before David died, he told Grandma Alice, "I would be a pianist for an evangelist, if one would take me."

Victor, the baby of the family, was just twenty-one years old when he was in a paper mill accident. While cleaning the rollers in the early morning hours, a coworker turned on the press not knowing that Vic was still on the catwalk between. Uncle Vic quickly tried to get to the end of the catwalk but slipped and became suspended in space between the rollers—his right foot caught in one and his left arm in the other. Hearing Vic's screams, the coworker turned the machines off and ran to get help.

When the EMS and doctors arrived, the emergency team physician had to amputate Uncle Vic's left arm with minimal anesthesia just to remove his upper body out of one of the rollers. In Vic's traumatic state, additional anesthesia would have killed him. Vic had a long wait until the paper mill mechanics arrived to disassemble the other roller to free his right foot. Vic almost bled to death, but God graciously saved his life for His purpose and for His glory.

After spending a year in the hospital, Uncle Vic went on to earn a doctoral degree in psychology. His greatest passion, due to some depression himself and witnessing all the mental disorders in the family, was to become an advocate for those who suffered with it. He has also interestingly helped many overcome addictions through self-hypnosis. I owe Uncle Vic a great deal of gratitude for being there for me in some of my darkest hours during Jonathan's illness, answering many of my questions regarding the disease.

As you look at the Garlock children and the preceding generations, mental illness, alcoholism, suicide, and creative minds abound. Jonathan's great-

great-grandfather was a preacher who unfortunately turned to alcohol for depression. In rages while intoxicated, he would beat the children with horse whips. Once while intoxicated, he threw Jon's great-grandfather Eddie into the snow from the second story window of their home.

Jonathan's great-great-grandmother, Jessie Ward Garlock, was a poet and musician. Creativity can be dated all the way back to the 1800s on the Ward side of our family. One ancestor, Henry Ward Beecher, was a famous public spokesperson of his era, often credited with helping set in motion the Civil War with his criticism of slavery. His sister, Harriet Beecher Stowe, wrote the popular *Uncle Tom's Cabin*.

On Jon's grandmother's side of the family, Flora Jean Fox Garlock came from a family very gifted musically and also familiar with mental illness. Great-Grandma Fox, was treated for depression with shock therapy. Other members of the Fox side of the family have also lived with various forms of mental illness, causing the unkind disease to appear on both sides of Jon's family.

I share all this to make the point that mental illness commonly runs in families, especially creative ones.

Mental illness often is genetic but can skip generations. Over the last one thousand years, it has been observed that mental illness has a tendency to run in some families, but not in others. Yet, like cancer, it can strike anyone, genetically disposed or not. Mental illness is not a respecter of persons.

God has given each of us brain chemicals that help account for our gifts and our individualities, from personality to intelligence. Our genetic make-ups are part of who God has created us to be.

For thou hast possessed my reins:
thou hast covered me in my mother's womb.

I will praise thee;
for I am fearfully and wonderfully made:

marvelous are thy works;
and that my soul knoweth right well.

My substance was not hid from thee,
when I was made in secret,
and curiously wrought in the lowest parts of the earth.

Thine eyes did see my substance, yet being unperfect;
and in thy book all my members were written,
which in continuance were fashioned,
when as yet there was none of them.

How precious also are thy thoughts unto me, O God!
How great is the sum of them!

(Psalm 139:13–17)

Yes, God knows us. He created us. He knows our length of days on this earth. He knows our struggles with sin. He knows our strengths as well as our weaknesses.

Extensive studies have been conducted about the tie between the history of mental illness in creative families such as Byron, Melville, Tennyson, Schumann, Coleridge, van Gogh, and Hemingway. Books upon books have been written about common threads of creativity that run through the lives of those with mental disorders. Most noteworthy of those in a religious realm are William Cowper, author of "There Is a Fountain" and Charles Spurgeon, London's most famous preacher in the 1800s.

Although creativity is not necessarily a precursor, often the affected individuals are creatively inclined—poetically, musically, and/or artistically, in that order.[1]

"We of the craft are all crazy," Lord Byron, a famous poet, said. "Some are affected by gaiety, others by melancholy, but all are more or less touched."[2]

---

[1] Dr. Adele Juda, 1949, *Lithium Encyclopedia for Clinical Practice*, 2nd ed. (American Psychiatric Press, 1987), 1468.
[2] R. George Thomas, *Edward Thomas: A Portrait* (Oxford University Press, 1908), 162.

William Cowper, who spent time in a mental asylum, wrote the following during one of his depressive episodes:

The weather is an exact emblem of my mind in its present state.

A thick fog envelops everything, and at the same time it freezes intensely. You will tell me that this cold gloom will be succeeded by a cheerful spring, and endeavor to encourage me to hope for a spiritual change resembling it. But it will be lost labour. Nature revives again, but a soul once slain, lives no more.[3]

Charles Haddon Spurgeon was called the "Prince of Preachers." Spurgeon himself suffered from chronic depression. Interestingly, the words of one of William Cowper's most famous hymns are etched on Spurgeon's tombstone.

There is a fountain filled with blood
Drawn from Immanuel's veins.

And sinners plunged beneath that flood
Lose all their guilty stains.

The dying thief rejoiced to see
That fountain in his day;

And there may I, though vile as he,
Wash all my sins away.[4]

Many people who have bipolar illness are brilliant as well as creative. What causes this? One holistic doctor we took Jonathan to explained the brilliantly creative brain phenomena in this way: the more intricate a machine is, the more that can go wrong with it. This may not be true, but it is interesting. At times people tell me they wish they had the musical abilities our family has. I tell them to be careful what they wish for. If they only knew the downsides. Being creatively talented is not always as glorious as it looks.

---

[3] Harold Nicholson, (1947). The Lloyd Roberts Lecture for 1947 on "The Health of Authors," British Medical Journal, 5.
[4] William Cowper, "There Is a Fountain," 1772.

Very intriguing is Genesis 1:1, which tells us that God "created" us. God is the "Lord of creativity" and has passed that gift onto us. I feel assured He understands the downsides of our sinfulness inherited from Adam and the complexities of the creative mind.

If you are interested in reading extensive accounts regarding the common threads of mental illness that run through the lives and generations of poets, musicians, and artists, Kay Jamison's book, *Touched with Fire: Manic-depressive Illness and the Artistic Temperament*, is an excellent source. In her book, Dr. Jamison shows extensive family trees of creative geniuses such as Lord Byron, Sir Walter Scott, John Keats, John Ruskin, and William Cowper. She is a professor of psychiatry at Johns Hopkins University School of Medicine and has a unique perspective in that she is not only an expert in psychiatry but also suffers with bipolar illness herself.

Top: Uncle David's funeral - L to R - Don, Ed, Grandpa Eddie, Vic, Elmer, Bob, Frank
Front Row: Eunice, Grandma Alice, Alice

Right: Uncle David - concert pianist

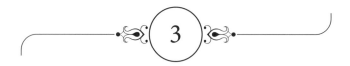

But I Didn't Marry a Pirate

August 1969

Ron and I meet while attending Bob Jones University. I am a sophomore in high school and he, a freshman in college. Ron first spots me as I run across campus in a cheerleading uniform. I first notice him as he was singing in my dad's vesper choir. A few nights earlier, I had literally dreamed of marrying a handsome, blonde-haired, blue-eyed boy. Ron and I soon begin dating and continue doing so for six years before tying the knot.

May 31, 1975

The organ chimes ring. One, two, three . . . eleven chimes mark the beginning of one of the most beautiful journeys of my life. On May 31, 1975, a thousand guests gather to witness my union with Ron Hamilton, my high school sweetheart. The Hamilton household is established.

January 1978

Three years into our marriage, while both teaching music at BJU, Ron begins having trouble reading the music over his voice students' shoulders. He assumes he needs eyeglasses. Bob Jones just announced that the following school year an optometrist will be offering free glasses to any faculty or staff member who requires them. Since we are going to be leaving the university the next year to write music and travel full time with my dad, we aren't certain if Ron will be eligible for the free glasses.

Ron writes a note to the Dean of Men to ask if he can be a part of the benefit. He does not hear back immediately. In the meantime, with my parents urging, I make an appointment with their ophthalmologist, Dr. George Cousar. When the time for this appointment comes, Ron still has not received any word back from the Dean's office.

We decide for Ron to go ahead and keep the Dr. Cousar appointment. Dr. Cousar is an ophthalmologist who at the exam does a final step of enlarging the eyeball. At the time optometrists do not include this step. Because of the enlarged eyeball, a tumor is discovered in the back of Ron's left eye.

Dr. Cousar excitedly calls me from the waiting area into his examining room. He shows me Ron's tumor through his telescope. By the irregular shape and greenish color of the growth, he explains to us the possibility of it being cancer. He cushions the news with the chance that what he has found might just be a popped blood vessel.

We next follow Dr. Cousar to his office where he immediately calls Dr. Bell, head of ophthalmology at Emory University in Atlanta, Georgia. The waiting period has begun.

The day following the Cousar appointment, Ron hears back from the Dean of Men. He is indeed eligible for the free eyeglasses. Amazingly, if Ron had gone for the free glasses that the university is offering, we likely would have never found the growth at the back of his eye.

I love it when God works on our behalf, even when we are not aware of His divine intervention.

Ron and I soon begin the first of many trips down to Atlanta, undergoing a series of tests that extends for four months. Ron is totally calm and trusting in God. Me? The months of waiting are traumatic. If Ron indeed has cancer, how extensive is it? We are informed that Ron's brain is the next place to which the cancer will metastasize. His life depends on the cancer being self-contained in the eyeball, or there will be nothing the doctors can do.

May 18, 1978

On May 18, 1978, Ron is rolled into the operating room for surgery. During the operation, if the doctors discover the growth is not cancerous, Ron will wake up with just a sore, blood-shot eye. If the growth is indeed a melanoma cancer tumor, as the doctors think, he will wake up without an eye.

Ron never loses his sense of humor. He asks the doctor as he is redressing his eye, "Will I be able to play tennis now?" The doctor assures him compassionately, "Yes, of course, you will." Ron replies, "Good—I never could before."

After four long hours in the waiting room, Ron's surgeon Dr. Bell finally comes in to see us. The good news is that Ron's tumor is self-contained in the eye and there are no signs of it in his brain. The bad news—the tumor is indeed melanoma, so the eye has been removed. My relief is so great that Ron will not die, losing his eye seems miniscule in comparison.

I am allowed to stay in Ron's hospital room for the week following surgery. I sleep on a cot and crochet an entire quilt during the time. Several days into recovery, Dr. Bell comes in to check on Ron's progress. He also wants to show me how to clean the empty eye socket. The bandage he removes over the left side of Ron's face is at least four inches thick.

Dr. Bell is so proud of his work. As he shows me all the clean incisions behind the former eyeball, I start to faint. Fortunately, his nurse catches me before I hit the ground. Ron says it will not be a problem; he will do the necessary cleaning.

My mother brings me a favorite snack to the hospital, Ocean Spray™ cranberry juice and Wheat Thins™. As much as I love both, they don't sound appetizing at all. My sister-in-law Nancy suggests to me that I might be pregnant. I think, *No way.* I find out, however, after returning home to Greenville that, sure enough, I am. God, as He always does, gives blessing out of trial. Eight months later we name our blessing "Jonathan," which means "gift from God."

The duration of waiting for Ron's surgery and possible fate is one of my most trying times of faith. It helps me, however, prepare for another extremely difficult time just eighteen years later, for which I am glad I have no foreknowledge.

Ron's losing his left eye is not the end of the story. After the final bandages are removed, Dr. Bell tells us to go to a drugstore and get a plastic pirate patch. Ron does just that. It is not long, however, before Ron ditches the plastic version and makes his own out of an old leather boot and some elastic string.

May 25, 1978

Kids from our home church gather around Ron at the end of that first Sunday service back home. When they ask what happened, Ron says, "I guess I'm a pirate now. In fact, you can call me Patch the Pirate." The kids love this and run back to tell all their friends. Soon there is a whole shipload of kids running towards the front of the church shouting, "Ahoy, Patch the Pirate." The name sticks.

I don't clearly remember the original eye patch Ron makes, but a year later, our friend Bob Cook offers to make him another one. Bob traces a pattern for the new patch and beautifully crafts it out of soft leather, adding etching around the edges. Ron continues to wear this same patch today. Although weathered and complete with patina, it has become a true symbol of Patch the Pirate.

June 1978

The summer after Ron loses his eye, Ron and I live at the Wilds Christian Camp in North Carolina. We lead the music program. In June, Ron and I make a trip to Michigan for him to receive a new prosthetic eye. We return back to camp, however, with Ron still liking to wear the eye patch better. While taking a walk down the main dirt road at camp, Ron and I discuss his eye patch. I say, "But I didn't marry a pirate." He responds, "You will have to accept that preferring the patch is the little kid in me." Later, when looking back, I cannot imagine him any other way.

August 1978

Ron and his sister, Marty, and I begin traveling with Dad in the following fall of 1978. Dad also purchases a home for Majesty Music right off the campus of Bob Jones. Ron and I live on the first floor. The second floor consists of a bedroom and bath where Marty lives. The basement becomes the office headquarters for the ministry/business. Marty loves and plays with our Jonathan. He calls her "Tee-tee."

What God began in 1978 is still ministering to thousands of children today in 2021.

Very soon Ron and I begin producing Patch the Pirate Adventure™ recordings. It is not long before he is being called Patch the Pirate by children everywhere. The first recording is called *Sing Along with Patch*. The Patch audios grow into full-scale, fun-character, adventure stories interwoven with original biblical character songs.

I am told that it is uncommon for anyone to survive melanoma in the eye. In fact, I talk to a woman whose husband has the same eye cancer, the same surgery, and is told that the cancer is self-contained. One year later, however, he succumbs to the cancer that has traveled throughout his body. I am overwhelmed by the reality that this could have been Ron's story.

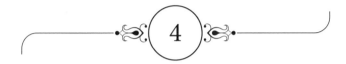

Jonathan—Our Gift from God

11:00 a.m., January 18, 1979

I have now gone exactly through nine months of pregnancy. Today, January 18, is going to prove to be one of the best days of my life as well as one of the worst.

Although Ron and I have gone through Lamaze classes, I am totally unprepared for what lies ahead. I awaken about 7:30 a.m. with mild labor cramps. I start timing them—five minutes apart. I get Ron up. Maybe we should head to the hospital.

We arrive at Barge Memorial Hospital on the campus of Bob Jones University around 9:30 a.m. At this time, they are still allowing childbirths, but only *natural* because there is no anesthesiologist. My pains are about three minutes apart now and growing more intense.

I check in, don my hospital gown, and get situated in a private room. All is going as anticipated so far. I get my focal point established on the ceiling and am lying down with my knees up to my chest, breathing as instructed through each contraction. Ron sits quietly in a chair by my side.

At 10:30 a.m. the labor pains start becoming very acute when a contraction presents. I begin beating on Ron's chest with both fists in rhythm while chewing on ice chips in the same rhythmic pattern. I try to keep my eyes centered on my focal point.

The head nurse comes in and tells me I need to put my knees down and lie flat on my back. I beg her to let me keep my knees up. She comes over and with one fell swoop shoves my knees down to the bed, single-handedly breaking my water. This was both shocking and painful.

The nurse tells me to settle down—I could be like this all day. I respond, "Well then, you'd better shoot me." What we both don't know is that I am in transition, the time in delivery when labor pains are the worst. Transition usually lasts no more than twenty minutes and occurs right before the baby comes. Another nurse says, "I see the baby's head. Get the operating bed, we're going down to OR."

As the bed arrives, two nurses have the daunting task of moving me from the bed I am on over to the operating bed. Jonathan is trying to deliver himself without our help. There is a problem. His head is turned posterior, which means upside down. I am in agony. My mom and dad are standing outside my hospital room door listening to me scream. (They say *scream*; I say, *moaning very loudly*. If you want to hear *scream*, I can do *scream*!)

I see Mom crying as they roll me past her and down the hall to the elevator. We finally enter the OR on the first floor. Jonathan's head turns to the proper position, which I feel intensely, and he is born. I've never seen so many people move so quickly. Jonathan makes his official entrance into the world at 11:00 a.m., January 18, 1979. All is done, and all is well. Our sweet little baby boy has arrived—Jonathan Campbell Hamilton.

Jonathan is named after my brother Randy, whose full name is Jon Randall, and after his great-great-grandmother Sadie Mae Campbell, my Grandma Alice's mother.

Ron writes a song for our new baby boy.

> *Jonathan Campbell Hamilton*
> *You bring Mom and Daddy lots of fun.*
>
> *The name of Campbell brings the best to you.*
> *Campbell makes the best babies, too.*
>
> *The days are shorter, the nights are longer,*
> *Purses lighter, but the future's brighter.*
>
> *Jonathan Campbell Hamilton,*
> *You bring Mom and Daddy lots of fun.*
>
> *Just like soup needs a sandwich, too*
> *The Hamiltons need a baby just . . . like . . . you.*

The first two weeks of Jonathan's life are a dream. Unfortunately, it is short-lived as colic sets in. Not just any colic, but the spewing kind that occurs every two hours directly following his feedings. Due to losing his entire milk consumption each time he nurses, he remains continuously hungry.

Ron and I, as well as other family members, take turns pacing with him up and down our hallway. I distinctly remember thinking, "Is this what having a baby is like?" I also cannot leave him at home without me because he is unwilling to take a bottle of formula. As predicted, Jonathan's colic ends in about four months. But what a four months they are.

In February, Ron, Jonathan, and I begin traveling to churches by way of our friend Carl Blyth's motor home. We perform concerts, and Ron preaches. One Sunday afternoon, when Jonathan is about six months old, he develops a temperature of 103 degrees. I am worried sick. We take Jonathan to the emergency room. The doctor there doesn't know what is causing the fever but puts him on an antibiotic anyway. I call our pediatrician, Dr. James Sightler, who agrees to meet us at his office first thing the next morning. We head back to the church to lead the evening service in song and for Ron to preach.

After the final "amen," Ron, baby, and I pack up our motor home and head toward Greenville, driving all night to get home in time to meet with our doctor. When Dr. Sightler checks Jonathan the next morning, he tells us that the antibiotic the emergency room doctor has put him on is exactly the right thing. We are so grateful to God for taking care of our son.

May 1979

Five months after Jonathan is born, I become pregnant with our second child. Due to the difficulty of writing and publishing sacred music, traveling, and being a mother of a baby with another one on the way, Ron and I decide for me to go off the road. Gina Young takes my place as pianist and starts traveling with Dad, Ron, and Marty.

July 27, 1980

Eighteen months and nine days following Jonathan's birth, our sweet little Taralee Joy is born.

Dad sells the home where we are living and buys a new office space for Majesty Music on Wade Hampton Boulevard. Ron and I purchase our own personal home in the historic Earle Street area. While I am still in the hospital with newborn Tara, Ron moves our family's belongings to our new home. When Tara and I leave the hospital, we enter our new living spaces crowded with unpacked boxes and an unfinished kitchen. The very next day, Ron, Dad, and the musical team take off in Dad's airplane for a six-week tour on the West Coast. I am left home alone with 18-month-old Jonathan and newborn Tara. Obviously, I survive.

Tara gets a song written for her as well.

> *How I love you in the morning, when the day has just begun.*
> *How I love you in the evening, at the setting of the sun.*
>
> *Whether waking or sleeping, you're the dearest one to me.*
> *How I love you, little lady, little lady Taralee.*

When our son Jonathan is two years old, a friend of ours who Jonathan calls Bobo, decides to dress like a bunny and surprise him with an Easter basket. Keep in mind that Bobo is over six feet tall. With bunny ears, he towers over eight feet. At the time of Bobo's entrance, Ron and I are out for a special dinner at McDonald's. Our friend Louise Mason has come over to babysit. When Bobo knocks and Louise opens the door, Jonathan is confronted by an eight-foot-tall rabbit. He starts flailing and crying. He cannot be consoled. Bobo finally has to leave, his surprise terribly foiled.

When Ron and I arrive home a little later, Jonathan is still "glued to the ceiling." As Ron tries to comfort him and puts him to bed, Jonathan cries, "The giant bunny is going to get me. The giant bunny is under the bed." Ron pats Jon's arm and prays. He then tells him to scoot over so Jesus can lie down beside him. Jonathan finally falls asleep.

A few years later, upon remembrance of this story, Ron writes the song "How Can I Fear." If you look in a hymnbook, you will see that every melody receives a tune name. This name is usually found at the bottom righthand corner of the hymn in all capital letters. The purpose is that one melody can have multiple lyrics scribed to it. Ron calls the tune name for "How Can I Fear": JONATHAN.

How Can I Fear?
by Ron Hamilton © 1984 by Majesty Music, Inc.

When shadows fall and the night covers all,
There are things that my eyes cannot see.
I'll never fear, for the Savior is near;
My Lord abides with me.

Refrain

How can I fear? Jesus is near.
He ever watches over me.
Worries all cease; He gives me peace.
How can I fear with Jesus?

When I'm alone and I face the unknown
And I fear what the future may be,
I can depend on the strength of my Friend—
He walks along with me.

Jesus is King; He controls everything.
He is with me each night and each day.
I trust my soul to the Savior's control;
He drives all fear away.

April 27, 1982

Twenty-one months after Tara is born, our adorable Alyssa enters the world. Jonathan is blonde, Tara brunette, and Alyssa redheaded. Ron says we can stop now because we have one of every flavor.

April 17, 1989

God brings us joy again, for our quiver is not quite full. Our smiley and bouncy Megan comes along on April 17, 1989. One year after Megan is born, I become pregnant again. I will never forget it. During the first ultrasound, the nurse tells me she cannot find the heartbeat. I don't remember if Ron is with me for this revelation or not. What I do remember is the pain that pierces through my heart.

I return to work at Majesty Music following the ultrasound. I recall it with perfect clarity, because Ron has just written a children's song entitled "Cherish the Moment." I am in the midst of writing a piano accompaniment for it. Tears will not stop rolling down my cheeks as I arrange, the lyrics reminding me of our loss.

The text of "Cherish the Moment" serves as a reminder to parents everywhere to hold onto every moment we have with our children. We do not know in advance how long they will be loaned to us on this earth.

Cherish the Moment
by Ron Hamilton © 1990 by Majesty Music, Inc.

Read my book, rub my back; Mommy, listen to my prayer.
Let me sit in your lap. Daddy, fly me through the air.
Throw a ball, make a snack; can we go to the park?
Tuck me in, hold me close; I'm afraid of the dark.

Refrain

Cherish the moment; soon you'll be apart.
Cling to the memory; clasp it to your heart.
Soon comes the day when You'll have no child to hold;
So, cherish, cherish the moment.

Sing a song, play a game; swing me high in the air.
Ride a bike, fly a kite; how I love the times we share.
Hold my hand, hug my neck; Daddy bounce me on your knee.
Come and sit by my bed; Mommy, rock me to sleep.

Think ahead to a time when your little ones are grown;
Hold them tight, don't lose sight of the blessings you have known.
Think ahead to a time when your little boy's a man
And you'd give anything just to hold him again.

The last stanza of this song becomes prophetic.

June 7, 1993

Our family is still not complete. Three years later, June 7, 1993, God tags on our caboose, sweet Jason. I love our little clan. It is like having two families in one. The three older children help with the younger two. Unfortunately, none of the other children after Jonathan and Tara get an original baby song written for them.

May 21, 1989

Dear Jonathan

I love you. You are nice and kind and so many other good things. You are the best brother in the whole wide world! I hope you have a good day tomorrow. Thank you for all you have ~~done~~ done to me.

Love,
Taralee Hamilton

You are
Kind   sweet   obedient
thoughtful
thankful
content

Top: Jonathan (age 10) and Tara (age 9) are very close

Right: Jonathan (age 8) gives all his money at Christmas as a surprise to Ron and me and Tara (age 7) matches his gift

To Dad from Jonathan
I ♡ you
and from Tara

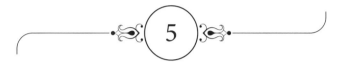

Early Years

1981

When Jon is two years old, he becomes PeeWee Pirate on our audio *Patch the Pirate Adventures*™. We have been asked if Jonathan at any time disliked his pirate name. I don't remember him ever saying he minded. I do recall, however, his friends at school reprimanding those who called him PeeWee, saying, "His name is Jonathan."

Jonathan seems to embrace his name and pirate character throughout his childhood. All of our children—PeeWee, Pixie, Peanut, Princess, and PJ seem to enjoy their roles. Alyssa, however, occasionally jabs that if only she wasn't the middle child, she could have been "Princess" instead of "Peanut."

1982

When Jon is three years old, on the *Patch the Pirate Goes to Space* story, he prays the sinner's prayer as PeeWee asking Jesus into his heart. This child's petition to God is so sweet. We are told many children have come to Christ by listening to this prayer. Praise God.

1983

Growing up, Jonathan is like any other active young boy. He spends hours in our backyard creek finding snakes and bugs. He loves playing soccer and slides on mattresses down our basement stairs. He accepts Jesus Christ as his personal Savior when he is just four years old.

He loves to be funny and sometimes even annoying! He remains a challenge to discipline; but by second grade, Ron and I feel that the disciplining has paid off. He becomes obedient and sweet.

When Ron and I gave our firstborn son the name of Jonathan in 1979, I never wanted it to be shortened to Jon. However, as already mentioned, this does not happen as I had hoped.

For some reason, Jon as a toddler has trouble saying his r's. Mom's dog Kipper is "Kippuh." Tara and Alyssa pick up on this little quirk as well.

I think I should mention that during our children's growing up years from 1980 through 1993, Ron continues traveling with Dad during the school months. Many weeks Ron is gone for music seminars, leaving Tuesday morning and arriving back home mid-Saturday. I am in total agreement with Ron's traveling ministry, but these years are challenging for me. I become the main disciplinarian, caregiver, and playmate to our children during those few years.

I have a humorous memory in retrospect when Jonathan is four and Tara three. While I am on the phone in the kitchen, they give each other a haircut on the back patio. Tara cuts some of the hair on top of Jonathan's head clear to the scalp. I end up taking him to get a buzz. Jonathan cuts one of Tara's pigtails completely off above the rubber band. She ends up with a pixie cut. I can't remember if the name "Pixie Pirate" is before or after the fact. Either way, it is apropos. What I do remember is feeling like I have failed as a mother. If I had only known at the time how minor this incident was.

1984

Jonathan and Tara go to Southside Christian School for kindergarten. Their beloved four-year old kindergarten teacher is Cookie Altizer. The children love her. Cookie tells us that when Tara gets into her class the year following Jonathan, Tara is as quiet as a mouse. She, however, after one semester realizes that Jonathan is not around to do all the talking for her. Now with her newly discovered voice, Tara won't stop talking.

1985

I try to be Jon's piano teacher. We have our weekly lesson after Jonathan gets home from school. He has had enough of sitting still and listening for the day, causing him and me both to end our lessons in tears. Consequently Jonathan, as well as Tara and Alyssa, begin taking piano lessons from Mrs. Muriel Murr, my piano teacher when I was growing up. Mrs. Murr is a blessing from above and the sweetest children's piano teacher God ever created.

1986

In second grade Jonathan enters a song writing contest. He writes and submits a song trilogy called *The Animal Suite:* "Baby Chick Shuffle," "The Donkey Two-Step," and "The Turtle's Last Dance." We find out afterwards that Dr. Dwight Gustafson, a friend and well-known composer, is one of the six judges but does not know the names of the contestants. Jon wins first place in the competition.

Little did Ron and I know how Jon would later use his gift of songwriting. I start dreaming that Jon will be able to take over Majesty Music someday. He certainly seems to have the gifts that it takes.

1988

Jonathan's best friend growing up is Jason Hotchkin. Jason is a good, sweet, very athletic kid. He later goes on to play soccer professionally. We love it when Jason comes over to visit. Apparently, as I only recently learn, the two of them get into some pretty rambunctious boys' shenanigans, like knocking on neighbors' doors late at night when they are supposed to be in bed. After knocking, they run and jump over bushes to escape.

1989

When Jon is ten years old, our friend Bill Lewis builds a deck off the back of our house. Bill tells Jon if he helps him clean out his truck, he will build him a swing over the creek. This is all the motivation Jonathan needs. Countless hours of fun end up being spent on this swing.

Another friend, Kent Hovind, known as the Dinosaur Man, offers to build a spring swing with Jon's help. This swing is hung from a tree in our front yard. A wooden seat is attached to an old set of garage-door springs. The kids love bouncing up and down as they swing.

One day, as Jon is playing in the woods across the creek in our backyard, he stirs up a bees' nest. I'll never forget him running up to our front door screaming. He is covered with over three hundred sweat bees. They stick to his clothes and onto his body underneath his clothes. I go and grab a broom while Ron takes off Jon's outer layer of clothes. We scrape the bees off his skin with the broom as fast as we can. Forever after that Jonathan is deathly afraid of bees.

Jon and Tara have a good friend, Cara Davis. She comes over often to play. One such time, Jonathan coaches her to climb up a ladder outside our second-story sun porch to knock down a spider web with a broom. He promises to hold the ladder. While she is up there, a swarm of bees suddenly flies down towards Jonathan. He runs, leaving Cara stranded. So much for being her support. The ladder is unstable for a few seconds but unbelievably remains upright. She is fortunately not hurt.

1990

Even as a young kid, Jonathan has a desire to win his neighbors to Christ. He plays after school with a neighbor boy, Michael Tally, who lives down the street. When Jon is in the sixth grade, he is able to lead Michael to the Lord. As I have been reading in Jonathan's journal, he never stops praying for Michael by name. I recently learned that Michael still lives in the same house on the same street and is involved in Bible studies. Praise God.

Jonathan also leads another neighbor boy, David, to the Lord in our living room. These remembrances touch this mother's heart.

Bottom line, Jonathan is a normal young boy—very active, stubborn, and loves to be funny.

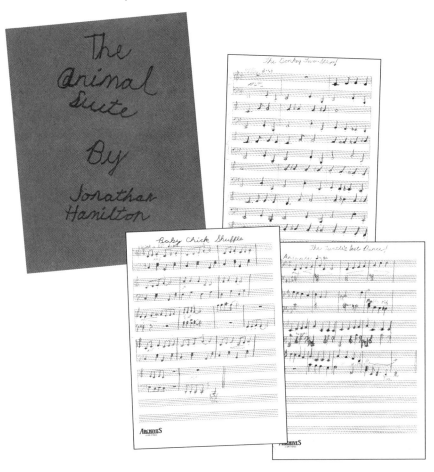

"The Animal Suite" by Jonathan Hamilton (2nd grade)—the three piano pieces he composes and wins first place in a Greenville Music Competition: 1. The Donkey Two-step 2. Baby Chick Shuffle 3. The Turtle's Last Dance

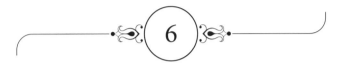

Challenging Teen Years

1991–1992

When Jonathan turns thirteen years old on January 18, 1991, Ron holds what is the equivalent of a bar mitzvah for him. Ron has become very intrigued with Jewish law and practices. He has brought back a menorah from a Holy Land trip, and our family lights its candles every New Year's Eve as we make New Year's resolutions.

A bar mitzvah is held for Jewish boys when they turn thirteen, portraying their coming of age religiously and legally. We invite every family member on both sides to be a part of the ceremony. Ron orders a T-shirt for Jon with "I Am a Man" imprinted on the front. The resulting family gathering with all the uncles giving words of wisdom to Jonathan is meaningful to all.

Jonathan, as has been demonstrated so far, remains physically active through junior high and high school. Our family continues living at the Wilds Christian Camp for a number of summers as Ron and I direct the music. Our children enjoy the benefits of spending long hours in the great outdoors during these months.

Jon is fearless. He loves diving off the top of the Second Falls and off the middle stone ledge at the 125-foot Fourth Falls. He enjoys going tree climbing with his friend Brian Olsen—and not just ordinary tree climbing. We are talking about one-hundred-foot-tall trees. I guess Jonathan could be categorized as a daredevil. (I really don't like that term, but you know what I mean.)

Back at junior high school, Jon loves to run and wins track competitions. He enjoys doing acrobatics on trampolines and performing tricks off diving boards with his cousin, Jeffrey Greene. Jon and Jeff are tight buddies.

Because of Jon's love of animals, he has multiple pets. But can he have normal pets like other kids? Are you kidding? What pets do we have in our home? An iguana, a flying squirrel, a cockatiel, and several snakes.

Our friend, Steve Allen, (and I use the term "friend" loosely) sends Jonathan several baby snakes with Ron on Dad's plane after a seminar held in Michigan. I beg Ron not to allow them into the house, but to no avail. Ron assumes I will get used to having them around. I am so fearful they will get loose. And get loose they do, while Ron is out of town traveling no less.

One such time, our friend Gary Emory and his kids come over to search under every bed and in every closet for the loose snakes. (Rachelle recently reminds me that it is mostly Gary that does all the searching. She and Alyssa, being deathly afraid, hide in Alyssa's room.) During the search, all the contents of each closet is thrown out into the bedrooms. Gary leaves me with a mess—and without success. Thank you, Gary!

The next morning, I wake up to find one of the snakes slithering down the hall. I yell out, "Praise the Lord!" Jonathan comes immediately to rescue the snake, or should I say to rescue me? Who knows where the other snakes end up? I have a recurring nightmare they crawl into the heat ducts only to mature, have babies, and come back to haunt me.

On one more occasion, another of Jonathan's pet snakes escapes out of the holding jar Jon has created as he cleans the terrarium. Ron, of course, is again traveling as Patch. Megan is a baby in the crawling stage, and I am horrified of the snake slithering onto her little body. I myself am afraid that the snake will slither onto my body.

I sleep with my arms held snugly by my side. I am afraid if I let one dangle over the bedside, the snake will crawl up my arm. Ironically, when Ron arrives home from his trip, we find the snake curled up on a piece of carpet under our bed—a carpet that Ron uses to keep his packed suitcase on.

In middle school, Jon continues to enjoy being funny—and annoying. He loves to talk. One memory distinctly stands out in my mind. Ron and I attend the first middle school parent/teacher conference for Jonathan. It does not end well. The teacher in the very first classroom is not happy with Jonathan.

Ron and I are fully aware that Jonathan is not perfect; but when not one positive word comes out of the teacher's mouth, I feel totally defeated and hurt. I tell Ron he is going to have to finish the rest of the conferences by himself, while I go to the car. I don't blame the teacher, as I'm sure Jonathan is a handful. Ron continues the rest of the parent/teacher conferences by himself.

One of Jonathan's friends tells us about a group of kids including Jon eating lunch at a Burger King™. They were on an eighth-grade class trip to Williamsburg. Two older ladies come in and sit down at a table near them. Jonathan says loudly enough for them to hear, "Hey Cheryl, do you think your parents know about us running away yet?" The kids get a laugh out of the looks they receive. Another friend, Lisa, remembers Jon giving her a bottle labeled "Diet Bubble Bath" for her birthday.

Jonathan, unfortunately, goes through the second half of his eighth-grade year in some rebellion. Late in the school year, Ron gets a phone call from Kmart. Their camera has caught Jonathan stealing. We know Jon has some issues, but this discovery is a shock—almost a catalyst moment, recognizing some serious behavior. Ron and I take Jonathan to the store and meet with security, who read him the riot act. He is fortunately a minor and doesn't need to spend any time in detention or prison. Jonathan is assigned a few months of community service.

Ironically, the same day we learn of Jonathan's stealing, we sit at the junior high school awards ceremony where our daughter Tara is given a citizenship medal. You learn to take the bad with the good.

Jonathan and his sister Tara are great friends, but unalike. In one of Jonathan's papers for school he writes:

> My sister Tara and I are vastly different when it comes to temperament. Tara has always been a very patient individual. I, on the other hand, have always been the kind of person who cannot wait for anything or anyone. She also has always been very laid back in nature and does everything slowly and thoughtfully. In contrast, when it comes to doing a job, I do it as fast as I can, just so I can get the job finished.
>
> My sister is not the type to get angry. In fact, I don't think I have ever seen her lose her temper. I wish I could say the same about myself. It is a daily struggle for me not to lose control of myself. I believe that my sister and I are as different as two siblings can possibly be.

September 1993

In 1993, Ron makes the decision to discontinue most of his traveling so he can spend more time with our children. A music pastor position comes available at Calvary Baptist Church in Simpsonville, just twenty minutes from our home. Ron candidates for the position, and we are soon happily busy leading the church music program. Ron's coming off the road is one of the best decisions we make. In the coming days, our family is going to very much need him.

In high school, Jon loses interest in piano, so we allow him to quit lessons. This is good timing, because later on in college, when he is ready and motivated, he begins piano lessons again and progresses quickly.

Jonathan is bright, fun-loving, and popular. He continues to enjoy making others laugh. Studies at school are not at the top of his priorities. One classmate recounts Jonathan coming into Bible class wanting to borrow her Bible. He wants to quickly learn the memory verse before a quiz. She laughs when grading his paper because Jon invariably writes his own version of the verse.

I have received many stories from Jonathan's classmates on Facebook about his antics in school. These antics, along with being tardy, earn him quite a few demerits.

The final straw occurs at the end of his first semester of his sophomore year. He asks one of his friends, an exchange student from Korea, how to say "pretty legs" in her language. He later shouts these words to another female Korean student in the school's quadrangle. The recipient does not see it as humorous but instead, justifiably so, turns Jonathan in to the principal's office. The principal calls for Jonathan and us to come in to see him. This meeting is where we are told Jon cannot return for two semesters to the Academy. With very heavy hearts we leave the principal's office. What to do now?

January 1994

Ron and I are not sure what Jonathan is going to do for his "free" year. We discuss the possibility of me homeschooling him. Soon after his expulsion, however, the Don Elie family, sweet missionaries from Russia, visits our church. To make a long story short, Jonathan is invited by this family to go to Russia and live with them for a few months. Jon goes and has the opportunity to see how another nationality lives. He helps teach English in the public school. Jonathan soon learns that Russians are a serious people and certainly do not appreciate his sense of humor.

We appreciate all that the Elie family is doing for Jonathan. While there, he is able to spend hours in his bedroom developing his guitar skills and studying the Bible. He lives in Russia for about three months and becomes "fired up" to serve the Lord. This is a challenging life experience for Jon, but a good one.

From Jonathan in Russia:

> *Dad and Mom, I am having the best witnessing opportunities. Forty-one kids got saved last week, and this week in my conversational English classes, I went through how God created the heavens and the earth and the whole plan of salvation with every class I had; and if God keeps on working in their hearts (and I know He will), I'm confident that when I ask if they want to be saved next week, many will respond!*
>
> *I see God working in my own life as well as others and that is what makes it worth being here. I love both of you tremendously, and I pray and hope that God is working in your own hearts. Don't let a day go by without growing closer to the Lord. Make sure to remind Tara to go witnessing and to invite others. And PLEASE make time to take them. I love you both and miss you greatly . . . Please pray for me. I'm praying for you. Jon*
>
> *Heal me, O LORD, and I shall be healed; save me, and I shall be saved; for thou art my praise. (Jeremiah 17:14)*

After Jon leaves Russia, he is invited to go spend a few months with Paul and Theresa Bixby in Spain. The Bixby family takes Jonathan to visit beautiful Spanish castles. You might remember, Jonathan loves to climb. We receive pictures with Jonathan perched on top of a castle turret or wall. Yikes.

In Spain, he becomes close friends with Mike and Madelaine Dodgens. He enjoys babysitting for and playing with their three children.

Theresa Bixby tells of trying to coax Jonathan to wash his bed sheets. Jonathan replies, "But my mom only washes our sheets every few months." Horror. I didn't wash the sheets every week, but this was a bit of an exaggeration.

The few months Jon spends in Spain are good as well—all in God's plan to develop Jonathan into the man He wants him to be. Russia and Spain are big turning points for our Jonathan.

From Jonathan in Spain:

> *To my family . . . I've been sick these last couple days. It's my first time being sick away from you guys . . . I wanted to be able to have my mom bring me some donuts and get some movies for me and have Dad get mad at me because I was watching too much TV. When I was feeling pretty sick, I wanted my mom and dad and all of you; but the Lord really comforted me and showed me He was all I needed. I was just thinking last night, how awesome it is to be able to pray to God for hours at night and feel he's right there with you.*

I have letters saved in Jon's scrapbook written to him from his siblings and friends while he is overseas. One such birthday card stands out in my mind. All our kids have signed it with sweet notes. Jason's message to Jon grabs my heart:

> *"Dear Jon, I love you so much. I would die for you. Love, Jason"*

I am not sure where the nickname originates, but some of the letters I read from friends to Jonathan—friends like Dibet Hotchkin, Greg Blake, and my sister Gina—all address his letters, "Jon the Cool." Apparently, the name sticks from somewhere. Greg, hilarious as usual, signs his letter "Greg the Great."

Here is an excerpt from one of Jonathan's journals during his overseas stay:

> *I want to be an evangelist, but I learned tonight that God can also call me to be other things. I better not try to be what I want to be, even if it's something godly. I'd better be what God wants me to be.*

Another journal entry soon after reads:

> *I just went witnessing. It was awesome. Two people got saved. . . .*
> *Nothing encourages me more than to see someone come to Christ.*
> *. . . I want to make my Father glad. Both of them: heavenly and*
> *earthly. And the verse says "a foolish son is the heaviness of his*
> *mother." That's what I was last year, and I want now to make my*
> *father glad and my mom. I love my parents, and I don't want to*
> *do anything to hurt them.*

July 1994

In the summer of 1994, when Jon eventually comes home from Russia and Spain, he brings gifts for my parents, his siblings, and for Ron and me. Jonathan has exquisite taste. Our family gets a hand-painted chess set from Russia. Ron and I each get a Russian hat made out of mink. I also receive a beautiful 14 carat gold necklace with matching earrings. Ron receives a valuable sword from Spain. My mom gets a white silk woven shawl. Jonathan spends all his money on his family—very sweet.

Top: Jonathan with Philip and David Elie gathering daily groceries
Bottom: Jonathan in Spain enjoying family dinner time with the Paul Bixby family

Calm Before the Storm

August 1994

After Jon's six-month overseas sabbatical, he returns home a changed individual, dedicated to serving God.

Jon still has a semester of school before he can return to the Academy. Our dear friends, Ken and Mardi Collier, from the Wilds Christian Camp, have a son Aaron who is Jon's age. The Colliers graciously take Jonathan into their home. Jon goes the first semester of his junior year with the other Wilds staff kids to the public high school in Brevard, North Carolina.

I remember four stories about his high school experiences there.

- The Wilds kids ride a small bus every day to the public school in Brevard. Most of the kids scrunch down in their seats when passing other students on campus, embarrassed about riding on the camp bus. I am told that Jon is one of two who remains sitting upright and tall. (This is not a criticism of the other kids, because we all realize how easily embarrassed teenage kids can get.)

- In English class the students are asked to write a paper on any topic they want. When the assignment is completed, everyone reads their papers to the class. Jon writes his paper on creation and why the Bible is the Word of God. I am told that this earns Jonathan the respect from the other high schoolers—saved and unsaved alike.

- The high school music teacher loves Jonathan. She tells me he is talented, sweet, and very respectful. She says she sees Christ in him.

- Jonathan sings a solo for the end of the year school program. Connie Henry, head of the dining hall serving staff, writes Jon a note afterwards:

Jonathan, I just wanted to say how much I appreciated you singing your solo last week. I'm not sure how much courage that took for you to do that, but I do know it took courage just to sing a solo let alone sing such a strong Christian song at a public high school. Thank you for taking a stand for the Lord and for making a difference at Brevard High School. Keep shining for the Lord. In Christ, Connie Henry

January 1995

After attending Brevard High School with the Wilds staff kids, Jonathan is finally able to return to Bob Jones Academy the second semester of his junior year and for the entirety of his senior year. These are also good months for Jon spiritually.

One Sunday after an evening church service, our family goes through some unforeseen drama. Jonathan and Alyssa ride with two friends after a Sunday evening church service to a teen event at a church family's home. As the group of four are traveling back home afterwards, the brother who is driving veers slightly off the road. He panics and accidentally hits the accelerator instead of the brake. The car travels full speed into a tree and hits where Alyssa is sitting in the front passenger seat. Her head knocks out the side window and strikes a tree.

Jonathan and the teen who are sitting in the backseat bump heads. Jonathan is knocked unconscious for a few moments. Amazingly, Jonathan is the one who has reminded everyone to put their seat belts on before leaving the house. Fortunately, another car leaving the event is close behind them. They witness the accident and return quickly to the house to call 911. (Though the technology is there, smartphones had not become "all the rage" until the late 1990s.)

Two ambulances come. We are told Jonathan, still bleeding from his nose, sings hymns all the way to the hospital in one of the ambulances. Alyssa travels in the other, in critical condition.

Ron and I are called immediately. When we arrive at the hospital, we hear the medical team working on Alyssa in one of the curtained cubicles. As the head nurse asks me for my license, I hear one of the doctors say as Alyssa's pulse is dropping, "We're losing her."

My legs fold underneath me, and I collapse to the floor. Alyssa's ear is bleeding profusely, and the medical staff think it might be coming from her brain. I experienced at that moment the possibility of losing a child. Shock, fear, and unbelief flood over me at the same time. Her life flashes briefly before my eyes. The doctors are finally able to get her bleeding stabilized and roll her down for an MRI. Mercifully, the blood is instead coming from her ear and not her brain.

I stay with Alyssa overnight at the hospital. I remember the next day, as the nurse lifts Alyssa's head from the pillow, a huge clump of hay-like hair remains. We learn this hair loss is a result from the physical stress caused to her body. Gratefully, the only long-lasting repercussion Alyssa experiences, for about a year, is getting her words confused.

August 1996

Jonathan is now a senior at Bob Jones Academy. After his junior year, Jonathan is elected to be president of his senior class. If I could pinpoint the greatest passion of Jon's changed life, it is his desire to share the gospel and win people to Christ.

Jonathan goes soul-winning one to two times weekly to our Greenville downtown area—once with his friend, now evangelist, Jeremy Frazor, and once taking a group of Academy kids on his own. I remember one evening as Jonathan is downtown, he witnesses to a man who is obviously intoxicated. The man gets right up in Jonathan's personal space as he is speaking to him. Jonathan backs up. The man asks, "What's wrong?" Jon replies, "Well, your breath stinks." This is definitely the wrong thing to say, and Jon gets a good boxing to the ear.

A young exchange student from Bangkok, Thailand starts attending the Calvary Baptist Church youth group. Her name is Ong. Jonathan and Tara make friends with her. One day when she invites them over to her stateside home, they are able to lead her to the Lord. Ong becomes a part of God's family as well as a part of ours. When she returns to Thailand, she faithfully writes and sends us presents.

All in all, Jon finishes out his high school career at the Academy with flying colors. He is among the five percent selected for *Who's Who Among American High School Students*. He writes out his testimony for the class president's address at the high school graduation ceremony. Here it is as given:

> *When I think back upon my life, I always think on God's mercy and love for His children. God has given me so much. He gave me great parents, a great church, a great school, but I chose to rebel against these and follow my own way after my own lusts. In my ninth-grade year at the Academy, I started to turn from all I had been taught. I was reaching the age where I started to realize that I had to make my own choices about life and what I was going to live for.*
>
> *Unfortunately, I chose the road of my own pleasure and started the process of totally shoving God out of my life. I would just like to stop here and thank the Lord that He lovingly chastises His*

children to keep them from the total destruction and damnation of sin. I will not go into any detail of my sin, but I will say had it not been for the loving chastening hand of God, I would not be standing here before you today.

The Lord, through my parents, this school, and His own Holy Spirit brought me lovingly back to Himself. I only wish I could describe for you the peace that God can give when one gives himself wholly to God. I also believe that one cannot understand this peace, until he experiences it for himself. I would encourage any of you here today that are holding anything back from God, to give yourself totally to Him, because only by a pure and clean heart can one have true joy and peace.

The beloved teen pastor at Calvary Baptist Church during Jonathan's high school years is Tom Craig. I cannot say enough good about Tom. Our children love him. Ron and I are good friends with Tom and his wife Kim. Tom loves to tease, so he and Jon get along well. Once, Tom hides one of my high-heeled shoes. I have discarded them for some temporary relief between choir practice and the service. He gets quite a laugh as I frantically scramble to find it before I have to play the piano prelude.

Tom is ambitious in reaching teens for Christ at public high schools in the area. I remember several times an entire school football team coming to a Sunday evening service at our church. What a great example he is to our children. Tom, due to cancer, is no longer with us. He is enjoying Jesus's and Jonathan's presence.

After graduation, Jon receives a witnessing award at the end-of-the-year teen church service. His favorite solo that he sings at church, at a detention center, and at a BJA chapel program is Mary Lynn VanGelderen's song "Help Me Win the Lost".

I have recently received the following message from one of his high school friends, Becca Buiter:

May I just say that I was in Jonathan's 1997 BJA class. I had just moved to Greenville my junior year, and he was one of the first students who befriended me at school. I was shy, scared, and somewhat angry about moving across the country from Texas. Jonathan sat next to me in Buffie Payne's Economics class, and he would talk to me (sometimes during class) and just make me laugh. He was one of the ones who made me finally feel at home at BJA.

He also encouraged me to go witnessing downtown with him and some of his friends. I was a bit terrified—but I went because I admired what those guys and girls were doing. Jon really helped me start overcoming my fears of sharing the gospel, and he kept me from giving up when I got discouraged and experienced opposition from some of the people at the bus station or store owners on Main Street. He was one of my buddies during the NYC mission trip during our senior year, and I remember him praying for me that I would have boldness to witness on the subway. He was so bold and would share the gospel with almost everyone we passed. . . . Hearing you share his struggles and God's goodness had such a healing effect on my heart this evening. Thank you for your transparency.

Please don't stop telling your story. You see—Jonathan's life had a big impact on mine. No, he wasn't perfect even during those late high school years, but I saw Jesus in him—and he was a good friend. He taught me to care about souls. In the last two decades of my life, I have helped lead several teams to Africa to share the gospel, and now I lead a BJU team to China each summer—as long as the door stays open. That shy senior girl is no more.

God is so good! He used a wonderful young man with mental illness to wake me up and show me that I could be bold for the sake of His name. Thank you for your boldness! You are in my prayers.

Love, Becca

Because of Jonathan's soul-winning passion, he later writes a beautiful melody for which he asks Ron to compose lyrics about being willing to go and tell the world about Jesus. The result: "I Will Go." Jon's voice is very similar to his father's. This song ends up being the only song we have recorded of Jonathan singing in his adult years, so it is especially dear to my heart. Jon sings it as a duet with Ron on our *Songs of Home and Heaven* recording.

Thank you, God, for being good to us and placing Jonathan in our family.

I Will Go
Lyrics: Cheryl Reid and Ron Hamilton;
Music: Jonathan Hamilton © 2005 by Majesty Music, Inc.

See all the people crying out to know the Lord,
Searching for the simple truth given in God's Word.
Bound by chains of sin,
Longing for release—
Who will share the gospel now and bring them peace?

Refrain

I will go. I must obey—
For Jesus is the answer. I know He's the way.
He calls me now. His voice I know.
While there are lost who need to hear—
I will go.

Hear people crying. See the hurt in every face,
Finding only empty things in their downward race.
How will people hear?
Who will point the way?
Who will take the love of Christ and go today?

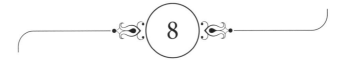

Mental Illness Strikes

September 1997

Jonathan begins his freshman year at Bob Jones University when he is eighteen years old. He chooses to become a music major, resumes piano lessons since dropping them in high school, takes trombone and voice lessons, and sings in Warren Cook's prestigious campus chorale. His freshman year at BJU goes smoothly, without a hitch.

I distinctly remember Jonathan sharing the dream for his future with me while standing at our kitchen sink at our 115 Chipwood Lane home. His dream is to become a music pastor at a large church and have a grandiose music program. Jon continues to go soul-winning once or twice a week.

At school, Jon loves to philosophize with his friends. He feels passionate about everything. One such friend I remember in particular is Erica Marcello, now Erica Henry, a pastor's wife in Michigan. I am going to let her describe her friendship with Jon at BJU and the Wilds in her own words:

After Jonathan received a soul-winning award one day in university chapel, it came up in conversation. He was so humbled that there was even an award for soul winning. He saw caring for people and their souls as a part of his everyday thought process and acted on it. Soul-winning for him was a normal part of life and his way of loving God. He gave all the glory to the Lord.

Jonathan was forgetful at times. He would walk off without his necessary books, leaving a pile. On more than one occasion, I found them and returned them to him. He asked, "How did you find them?" I answered, "It was your ball cap." His ball cap was unique to him and always sitting on top of his stack. One more thing. Jonathan never needed to be the center of attention. This is what cultivated my friendship with him, as we always found common ground—we both were content to be on the sidelines, just communicating about simple or authentic things.

I remember the summer Jon and I were counselors at the Wilds. During staff free time on weekends, we enjoyed singing around the piano in the fireplace room with two to three others. We had great conversations. Jonathan ALWAYS listened well—and listened in that caring kind of way that made you know he wasn't going to toss you away based on your thoughts or because the conversation would take too long. Our friendship was mutual, based on listening and praying for situations that we found ourselves pondering.

May 1998

The summer following his freshman year, Jonathan works as a counselor at the Wilds Christian Camp. He does well. Our friend Becky Kent tells me that her son has gone to the Wilds a number of summers, but Jonathan is the only counselor that he remembers. Jonathan makes a good impression on him. She recalls Jonathan wearing a T-shirt that first day of the camp week that says on the front: "I don't do windows." On the back it says, "But I'll clean your clock." Becky thinks this is perfect guy humor.

October 11, 1998

After summer camp, Jon begins his sophomore year at the university. In October he is asked to sing *Rejoice in the Lord* as a solo on the Sunday afternoon vespers program. Before he sings, he is asked to give Ron's "pirate" testimony. Jonathan does a wonderful job at two performances— 3,000 people attending each. Ron and I are so proud of him.

October 15, 1998

Jon is experiencing acne, so I encourage him to go see a dermatologist. I understand that there are medicines for problems like this. We go to the doctor appointment on October 15, and Jonathan is consequently put on an antibiotic. (I don't feel comfortable mentioning the name of the antibiotic on these pages. If you have any question regarding any medication, be sure to ask your doctor and then read the side effects carefully.)

After several weeks on the medicine, Jonathan begins demonstrating some strange behavior. He stops eating well and sits at the dinner table twirling the fork on his plate. He tells Ron and me that most foods don't taste good anymore.

Jon starts saying he feels extremely nervous all the time. Any action, even just saying "hi" to someone walking down the sidewalk at school, makes his heart pound like he is performing at vespers again. He tells us that life is mostly composed of nervousness and that love does not exist. He appears to be somewhat depressed, having occasional bouts of crying which is unusual for him.

When Ron or I walk by his bedroom at night, we see him staring at the book he is studying. When one of us walks by an hour later, he is still staring at the same page. What is going on with our son? We cannot imagine the cause of this dramatic change in Jon's life. We try to think of anything that is different.

Ron and I know something strange is happening. The only two possible culprits we can think of is the acne antibiotic or the allergy shots Jon has started taking. I call both doctor's offices and am told by the nurse at each clinic: it cannot be what they are giving him.

January 1999

On January 18, Jonathan's twentieth birthday comes and goes. Late January, I take another of our children to the same dermatologist Jon has seen. While there, I mention to the doctor about Jonathan's strange behavior. He says, "It's the medicine. Get him off of it." I say, "Are you sure? Your nurse told me it wasn't." He tells me again to get him off the medicine immediately. I say, "But—" The doctor cuts me off and tells me emphatically to get him off. I ask how long it will take after discontinuing the medication before he comes back to himself. The doctor responds, "Two weeks or so."

Well, we take Jon off, but two weeks come and go with no improvement. Jonathan not only doesn't come back to himself, but instead gets worse.

Also worth noting is that in late January Jon goes on a snow skiing trip with fellow college friends. Ron and I are told by his classmates that he has a hard fall on the ice and really takes a bad knock to his head. I have since learned that head trauma can trigger mental disorders. Is it possible Jonathan's illness is due to a reaction to medicine and head trauma? We don't know.

March 1999

Jonathan continues to not do well although carrying on with his sophomore year. We bring three different Christian counselors to our home, and all three believe that Jonathan's illness is a spiritual problem. Jonathan himself thinks his problem is because of some sin he has committed. I guess he convinces the counselors.

April 1999

Jon becomes more withdrawn and starts exhibiting a flat affect—his countenance is showing no emotion. We finally take Jonathan to our family doctor. Fortunately, he understands that Jonathan is in severe clinical depression. The doctor's mother had schizophrenia, so he is very familiar with illnesses that affect the mind. He puts Jonathan on an antidepressant, which unfortunately does not work.

Jon sleeps much of the time. He becomes more quiet and somewhat agitated, pacing back and forth in our living room. We discover it best to just leave him alone when his mind is troubled. Unfortunately, it is still not as bad as it is going to get. Unbelievably, Jonathan finishes out the second semester of his sophomore year with good grades. Whatever he gets, he learns while sitting in class, because he cannot focus on studying at home.

Jon is chosen to travel on a BJU ministry team for the fall of his junior year. He begins rehearsals in April. The team will not start their tour until the following August. We are hoping that certainly he will be better by then.

May 1999

Jonathan's sophomore year is over. After school is out, Jonathan, Tara, Ron, and I fly out to our cousin Kim Kliewer's wedding in Denver, Colorado. Jonathan and Ron sing two duets at the ceremony. After the wedding, a friend comments that Jonathan does well on the first song, but on the second song looks like he is going to murder somebody. Ron decides to take Jonathan off of the antidepressant he is on. Jon seems to get a little better.

Jonathan and our second child Tara have been planning on being counselors together at the Wilds Christian Camp for the summer of 1999. Believe it or not, we let him go to counselor/training week. Jonathan stares at the floor during sessions and barely talks to anyone. Ron and Ken Collier decide that being a counselor this summer is obviously a bad idea.

Some trials come and go. Some trials come and stay.

I keep hoping and praying that a miracle will occur—that Jonathan's illness will vanish and just be a bad nightmare. This, however, does not happen. Sometimes God allows us to see the good that He brings out of our trials. Sometimes He does not.

One of the biggest blessings of Ron's and my life has been the Patch the Pirate ministry—God working good out of Ron losing his left eye to cancer. With our Jonathan, however, his trial is making no sense to us. Jonathan's illness quickly becomes and continues to be the most devastating and challenging season of our life. Where is God's goodness to our son?

June 1999

Ron and I bring Jonathan home from counsellor-training week at camp and take him and our other three younger children to Florida for a two-week getaway. We go with a new antidepressant in tow. It is supposed to take two weeks for the medicine to even begin working at all and up to six weeks to know its full effect. In Florida, Jon mostly lies on the sofa with no expression. Ron coaxes him into some bike riding, swimming, and fishing.

While there, our family goes to the Pensacola Campus Church for a Sunday evening service and sit in the back of the balcony. Jon stares at the floor during the service. We hurriedly leave church afterwards in order to avoid seeing anyone. Jonathan does not have any dress shoes with him, so he wears a pair of Ron's, which are a tad big. Jonathan has trouble walking in them. Suddenly and without warning, he takes his foot and swings the shoe off his foot and across the parking lot. Extreme, over-the-top agitation is becoming an occasional problem.

You might imagine the anxiety I am experiencing regarding Jonathan. Ron, in contrast, remains resolute in his faith. He is a solid rock for our family.

We find out at the end of this vacation, on a Saturday in June at 2:00 p.m. to be exact, that Jonathan has not actually been swallowing the new antidepressant we are giving him. Ron and I hit an all-time low. I pray but feel that my prayers are hitting a brick wall.

Why do I remember the exact 2:00 time?

After we discover Jon has not been taking his medicine, we receive a phone call regarding a traumatic event. In North Carolina, our daughter Tara is traveling in the back seat of a car with several other counselors. The car goes off the road, rolls over several times, and ends up crashing into a tree. What time is the accident? 2:00 p.m.

The EMS are able to pull Tara out through the back window of the car, unscathed. What a rebuke to me. God is answering my prayer to help our family. I just didn't know what, for whom, and how.

Ron, kids, and I drive from Florida to home in Greenville on Sunday, the next day. Jon seems a little improved. Ron talks to our friend Ken Collier at the Wilds. Ron and Ken decide that if Jon will take his medicine, it will be okay for him to do a trial run, working on the Wilds cleanup crew. We send Jon to camp with the same antidepressant, which he promises to take.

Jon works for Doug Gorsline and alongside Doug's son Nathaniel. Andy Zale, a friend from school, is also on the crew. Jon does okay with work but paranoia issues remain as part of his existence. Nathaniel and Andy understand Jonathan is going through a tough time and give him support when needed. Thank you, guys! Your kindness means so much to my mother's heart.

Is God Really Good?

June 8, 1999

Our son is going through extreme mental trauma. The sadness and turmoil created in my heart and mind as a result has become debilitating. The journey through Jonathan's mental illness is a true-to-life lesson as to whether or not I actually believe in God's goodness.

I have held to the fact my entire life: God is good. I have seen it over and over again through Scripture, which I believe is infallible. Many beloved stories from its pages speak of His goodness. We have a beautiful world in which to live because God is good. Women, we are here because of it.

> *And the Lord God said, It is not good that the man should be alone; I will make him an help meet for him. (Genesis 2:18)*

God gives His children good things.

> *And they took of the fruit of the land in their hands . . . and said, It is a good land which the Lord our God doth give us. (Deuteronomy 1:25)*

An *if* and *then* biblical promise is: *if* we seek God, *then* God's hand will be upon us.

> *The hand of our God is upon all them for good that seek him. (Ezra 8:22)*

Goodness is a character trait of God. Jesus himself realized that there is only one who is good—God.

> *And Jesus said unto him, Why callest thou me good? none is good, save one, that is, God. (Luke 18:19)*

My husband Ron never questions God's goodness. I am more feeling oriented and want to sense it as well. Scripture should be enough. I, however, want to also feel in my heart and believe in the very depths of my soul it's truth.

I know in my head that God is good, but where is it in our son's illness? What is God's purpose and plan? No answer. No explanation. All that is left: to keep believing with the same faith—that the same God who turned Ron's cancer into a wonderful, joyous ministry will turn Jonathan's illness into something beyond our hopes and dreams.

I, therefore, go on an in-depth search to put an end to the agonizing in my mind about this critical issue standing at the foundation of my faith. The lengthy answer I discover in my quest is as follows:

- We live in a sin-broken world. The book of Ecclesiastes is the primary book of the Bible dealing with the topic. Our world is characterized by frustration, confusion, and the inevitability of it ending or us dying.

  > *And I myself perceived also that one even happeneth to them all. . . . For there is no remembrance of the wise more than of the fool for ever; seeing that which now is in the days to come shall all be forgotten. (Ecclesiastes 2:14, 16)*

- COVID-19 has been a reminder that we all will die. The frustration we feel in a sin-cursed world points us to the Son. Our lives would be meaningless without Christ.

  Yea doubtless, and I count all things but loss for the excellency of the knowledge of Christ Jesus my Lord. (Philippians 3:8)

- The good news is that Jesus Christ Himself was broken. Jesus tells us to remember His mutilated body as we observe communion. Jesus was broken so we could be whole.

  The bread which we break, is it not the communion of the body of Christ? (1 Corinthians 10:16)

The truth is we travel down many roads in this journey called life. Some roads are smooth, straight, and easy; some roads are bumpy, curvy, and difficult. Some roads are so smooth, the weather so balmy, and the journey so familiar, we can almost put our lives on autopilot. Some roads are so bumpy, the weather so stormy, and the journey unknown, that we have to keep our eyes glued to the road and to our GPS.

God created the world and everything in it to be beautiful and good. As I mentioned at the beginning of the book, Satan through Adam and Eve, by tempting them to eat of the fruit God forbade, brought sin into this world. And with sin—consequently bad things. It will serve us well to remember that Satan is the author of sickness, pain, sorrow, and death. Satan wants us to think that bad things happen because God is not good, but it is instead because Satan is evil.

I know through Scripture that there is a loving God, who sometimes allows Satan to test the children of God and who sometimes Himself decrees turbulence in our lives—to make of us what we can only be when He transforms the rough stone of our life into a polished diamond of beauty and value.

The diamond's fire and brilliance all come down to the skill of the diamond cutter. There are five steps involved in transforming rough diamonds into polished ones.

1. The planning stage is analyzing and evaluating how the diamond will be cut to get the best color and brilliance.

2. The cleaving/sawing stage is the use of cutting tools such as blades, saws, and lasers to cut the diamond into the desired shape.

3. The bruting stage uses a lathe as the main tool to rotate the diamond. A diamond loupe is then implemented to determine how to show off the stone's best attributes before it is polished.

4. The polishing stage starts with the diamond cutter creating each facet and then grinding those facets against a blade while spinning it. Afterward a lubrication-like oil is applied. Finally, the polishing wheel and pads are used to polish each facet. The polishing phase is a very time-consuming process and removes any coarse marks left.

5. The inspection stage is when the diamond is carefully evaluated for any external flaws left. If one is found, it can be sent back for further polishing. Following the inspection, each diamond gets a certification: excellent, very good, good, or fair.

Our lives are like diamonds—with God being the diamond cutter. The transforming process, with the skilled hands of God transforming the rough diamonds of our lives into stones of value and beauty, is in actuality the goodness of God. I feel like I must be receiving an extra dose of God's goodness through Jon's illness. I must have so many rough edges and external flaws, God has to keep sending me back for further polishing. I, through the process, hope to receive a certification of "excellent."

Would mankind have been better off to be created as robots, with no gift of choice, but no effects of sin either? I am personally glad that God did not create me to be so, but instead made me a human being with the ability to choose.

He knew in advance that Adam and Eve would sin, thereby bringing sin upon all mankind and necessitating God to send His only Son Jesus to earth, leaving the comforts of heaven to live in the midst of our fallen world, and then to die a horrible death on the cross in order to save men from their sin. This incredibly sacrificial offer of salvation is also the goodness of God.

God sees His only Son spat upon, ridiculed, and crucified to a cross. I've never had to experience that kind of horrific trauma. God understands when I ache for my child. What I know is that God makes sure His children will be fully recompensed for their suffering. He promises that He will turn our hurt into good and His pain into salvation through the gospel.

The Gospel

All that is required to be a child of God is to accept Jesus Christ as the gift of salvation—with no strings attached and no works of righteousness; believe that Jesus Christ is Who He says He is—the Son of God; accept that as the Bible teaches, Jesus Christ died on the cross and rose again; ask Jesus to forgive your sins and invite Him to come live in your heart. God made your way of escape from eternal damnation so simple. He will grant you salvation as He did for me and countless others. Jesus Christ will give you purpose in life and a promise of an eternal home in heaven with God. This salvation, my friend, is the goodness of God.

The goodness of God cannot be put into a box. My mind cannot fully comprehend the love of God. It is not possible that a human perspective of goodness portrays an exhaustive understanding of God's divine goodness. What we do know is that Satan is our enemy and brings bad things into our lives to ultimately destroy us. God is our friend and allows or sometimes decrees bad things into our lives to ultimately make us better.

He wounds, but he also binds up; He injures, but his hands also heal. (Job 5:18 paraphrased)

If God is indeed good, He must be wanting to do something extraordinary in my son Jonathan's life. God must love my suffering child more than I do. Trials must be more precious than gold for him too. I start believing God has something glorious for Jonathan despite and even because of his suffering. God loves all His children. He grieves when we become sick, and He heals when it is His perfect will to do so. I must accept everything.

I cannot always discern between what is good and what is bad. Whether I understand or not doesn't really matter in the larger scheme of what God is accomplishing in my life. I would like to be able to understand God's purpose, but this is not always possible. I cannot explain everything, but I can rest in the goodness of God.

Scripture tells me that "all things work together for good to them that love God, to them who are the called according to His purpose" (Romans 8:28).

As I begin to feel God's goodness, although I don't see it yet in our son's situation, it begins to wrap itself around me, comforting me, lifting me up, and giving me the strength to carry on. God's goodness becomes very real to me. The last thing Satan wants me to realize is its truth because the facts defeat his lies. What I do come to accept is that I must bless the Lord for all things.

Charles H. Spurgeon dealt with a lot of pain during his lifetime and some very crippling depression. He writes:

> *God is too good to be unkind, too wise to be mistaken, and when you cannot trace His hand, you can trust His heart.*[5]

This I do know, everything God allows His children to go through in this life is preparing them for the glorious life to come. God assures Christians:

> *I know the thoughts that I think toward you, saith the Lord, thoughts of peace, and not of evil, to give you an expected end. (Jeremiah 29:11)*

---

[5]*Charles H. Spurgeon Quotes, Wise Quotes*, paraphrase.

After all my digging, study of Scripture, and meditating, I conclude in my heart as previously done in my head: *God is always, only good.*

June 15, 1999

On the cleanup crew at the Wilds, Jon goes daily by the nurse's station to validate that he takes his medicine. By now, however, Jon is so suspicious of the medicine, he holds it under his tongue and spits it out when out of the nurse's sight. Jon works at the Wilds for the last six weeks of summer camp in the good outdoors. His mood seems to improve a little even without the medicine. His phobias, however, continue. When he swallows, he feels he is controlling others to subsequently swallow. He begins experiencing panic attacks and continues believing love doesn't exist.

The summer of 1999 is also when we start meeting with our friend Dave Pennington. Dave becomes a lifeline due to his knowledge of mental disorders. I call him frequently with my myriads of questions. He patiently answers all that he can. Dave also faithfully goes up to the Wilds to check on Jon and counsel with him. Jon, however, cannot be counseled out of his delusional thoughts. Jon stops praying and having his devotions, which is unusual for him. He is just existing. His motor movements are slowing down, and he exhausts easily.

August 1999

Jonathan comes home from the Wilds to begin his junior year of college at Bob Jones University. Due to his illness, he soon has to drop out. It becomes obvious he will be unable to travel on the ministry team. Dr. Darren Lawson, the Dean of Fine Arts, is very kind and understanding.

Because Jonathan's depression remains so severe, our doctor refers us to a Christian psychiatrist. At this point Jon's behaviors and erratic thought patterns need professional medical attention. Psychiatrists treat these types of illnesses all the time, and we need an expert.

Ron, Jonathan, and I end up at the office of a Christian psychiatrist. When we drive up, park our car, and see the sign indicating Office of Psychiatry, it is quite a humbling moment. We never have pictured ourselves going to a doctor such as this. We cannot imagine how it feels for Jonathan. This visit is to be the first among many. Under the psychiatrist's care, Jon is placed on a regimen of experimentation with countless medications, each requiring time to determine efficacy.

Let me say: It is very depressing to read about depression.

I begin reading everything on mental health that I can get my hands on. Ron wants me to stop all the study, wondering if learning about all the worse-case scenarios is really good for me. But I am determined to help my son in any way I can! Momma bear is fighting to protect her cub.

I am reminded constantly because of Jon's illness that I am not for this world but for the world to come. Everything I am going through here is in preparation for there. I want with all my heart for God to receive the glory, but I may not know the best way. I am certain glorifying God is also what Jonathan wants. We just have no idea how he will be tested for this to be accomplished.

When Abraham took Isaac to be sacrificed, he must have prayed, "Lord, please supply another lamb." Abraham had to wonder why God would give him something for which he had waited so long and then take it back. When and because Abraham offered Isaac to God, God fulfilled His promise to multiply Abraham's seed as the stars of the heavens.

Won't God fulfill His purpose for our family as He did for the family of Abraham? Jonathan's passion to win others to Christ will not be for naught but will be accomplished. Right? I am beginning to see a possibility that through Jon's illness, more people will come to Christ. Could this be so? I plead with God, *please help me understand Your reasoning in giving us this trial.*

At the same time Jonathan has to drop out of school his sophomore year, our Tara starts dating Ben Farrell. This is a highlight for our family.

Again, you take the bad with the good.

Jonathan continues living with us through the fall months.

I found these profound words from one of John Newton's letters:

> *Health is good while the Lord preserves it, and sickness is still better when he appoints it. He is good when he grants our wishes and multiplies our comforts; and he is good when he sends us trials and crosses. We are short-sighted, and cannot see how many and what important consequences depend upon every turn in life; but the whole chain of events are open to his view. When we arrive in the land of light, we shall have an affecting retrospect of the way by which the Lord our God led us in this wilderness. We shall then see that whenever we were in heaviness, there was a need-be for it. We shall then, I doubt not, remember, amongst our choicest blessings, those things which, while we were here, seemed the hardest to account for, and the hardest to bear. Perhaps we were sinking into a lukewarm formality, or spiritual pride was springing up, or Satan was spreading some dangerous snare for our feet. How seasonable and important at such a time is the mercy which, under the disguise of an affliction, gives an alarm to the soul, quickens us to prayer, makes us feel our own emptiness, and preserves us from the enemy's net. These reflections are applicable to all the Lord's people, but emphatically so to his ministers. We stand in the forefront of the battle. The nature of our employment exposes us to peculiar dangers; more eyes are upon us; our deviations are more observed, and have worse effects, both with respect to the church and the world, than if we were in private life. By our own sufferings we learn likewise (the Lord sanctifying them to that end) to sympathize with the afflicted, and to comfort them from the experiences we had had of the Lord's goodness and faithfulness to ourselves.*[6]

---

[6] J. Smith, *The Works of the Rev. John Newton* (London, 1821), 360. Retrieved from https://www.google.com/books/edition/The_Works_of_the_Rev_John_Newton/AoQxAQAAMAAJ?hl=en&gbpv=1&bsq=letters%20of%20John%20p.%20356%20impediments.

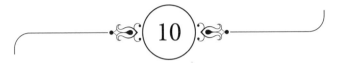

My Son, O My Son

December 1, 1999

A little over a year has gone by now since Jonathan first started showing symptoms of clinical depression after taking the antibiotic for acne. My heart is continuously gripped in pain. I cry to God, "My son, O my son."

Sarah Bennett is a dear friend who at the time lives across the street from us. She lives part-time in Greenville and the rest of the time in Haiti as a missionary. Sarah approaches me and tells me she has been impressed by God to help me get through this trial.

For most weekdays in December and throughout the year 2000, Sarah gets up at 4:30 a.m. and gets something from God's Word to share with me. I walk over at 6:00 a.m. to get encouragement and refreshment from God's Word. I call them my Morning Minutes. Sarah keeps a tissue box on her coffee table because during many sessions, all I can do is weep.

I want to inform you in advance that many of the Morning Minutes throughout this book contain commonly heard cliches. I was advised to remove them. I, however, have come to be encouraged by them as they relate to my journey. They are therefore remaining. You may call me the "Queen of Cliches" if you like, and I will not be offended.

Morning Minutes

As I cry, Sarah tells me it is okay. Tears are a way of melting a heart filled with grief. She uplifts my spirit, reminding me that God says there are bottles in heaven filled with our tears. Perhaps these tears will become diamonds that someday we can lay at the Master's feet.

Thou tellest my wanderings: put thou my tears into thy bottle: are they not in thy book?

(Psalm 56:8)

Sarah gives me two beautiful journals, every page of which I fill with gems of wisdom, pouring forth out of her mouth, emanating from Scripture. I'll never forget those days. Many words you will see in this book of spiritual encouragement originate from the Bible and pass through Sarah to me.

Sarah has been reading through a first draft manuscript of this book. She tells me, "I really don't think you should mention my name." I say, "Sarah, I am unable to do that. God spoke to you, then you to me. It wouldn't be right to take out the middleman."

Sarah tells me regarding Jonathan's illness:

Perhaps Satan is going before God like he did with Job saying, "If you do this and that to your servant, they won't love and serve you anymore." Satan may be telling God, "See all those songs Ron wrote praising You. If you test him, I bet You will discover he didn't mean it." God may be allowing Satan to test you and Ron. Stand firm.

I sometimes go over in the afternoon to pray with Sarah's mother who lives with her. Arshaloos, "Grandma Bell" as we call her, is a retired missionary to Haiti. Sarah and her mom are two spiritual mentors who are a godsend. Sarah continues her spiritual encouraging morning oasis for me the entire year of 2000, actually continuing into 2001 and beyond.

December 7, 1999

Morning Minutes

I tell Sarah that besides sorrow over Jonathan's illness, I am still occasionally fighting anger towards God. Why would God take a young, gifted man who wants to be an evangelist and/or music director and allow him to have this atrocious paralyzing illness? I question God, "Jonathan goes faithfully and shares Your gospel. Did You know there are not many young men who do this? You must have made a mistake. You have the wrong guy."

Grandma Bell tells me, "Shelly, Satan's got your number."

Sarah encourages me, "Never doubt God. When God wants to do something wonderful, He uses the difficult. When He wants to do something spectacular, He uses the impossible."

December 25, 1999

Christmas morning arrives. Jon seems to act more normal but does not eat all day. Four days go by without Jon eating or drinking. My dad, whom Jonathan loves, talks to him about needing to eat. Jon snaps and curses at him. This is not our Jonathan. He loves my dad and has never cursed a day in his life. Where in the world does this come from?

As I believe God's goodness, I am knocked down again with trouble, and subsequently doubt. I am getting dizzy. I mentally and emotionally go from depression trauma to spiritually, "I know God is good." Depression trauma to "God is good." Depression trauma to "God is always, only good." I feel like I am on a sped-up merry-go-round.

My spirit daily wars against my flesh. My spirit is willing, but my flesh is weak. Beyond question, there is a spiritual warfare in the very depths of my soul. I plead with God for Jonathan's healing, but it becomes more and more apparent this is not to be—at least not in the way I hope.

I can tell you from experience, anger towards God's omnipotence, rebellion towards what He is allowing in your life; and bitterness towards sickness, pain, and death is not a pleasant place in which to put yourself.

Jonathan's name means *gift*. God gives me a priceless gift of a child, and I become selfish, wanting to keep this gift for myself. I think I have given him back to God when he is born, but now I am faced with a where-the-rubber-meets-the-road choice. Am I willing to completely give Jonathan up if God asks it of me? God wants to know, "How much do you really love me? Are you willing to give me someone you love and cherish so much?"

Is God the one being unkind by asking? Or is it possible that His motives are truly pure and guided by knowing what is best for me and my family for all eternity? I want to believe the latter.

December 29, 1999

Because Jon is barely eating or drinking, Ron takes him for an evaluation at the Charter Mental Facility, one of Greenville's hospitals. We are all afraid Jon is dehydrating. The doctors decide to keep him. Various medications are tried during Jon's three-week, three-day stay. Some work. Some don't.

January 17, 2000

The day before Jonathan's twenty-first birthday, he still remains in the hospital. We are now over two years into Jonathan's illness. Sarah encourages me to write down everything I love about Jonathan. I journal:

Jonathan, You are not only our firstborn child,
but our firstborn son.
You are holy to the Lord.
You are both grandparents' firstborn grandson.
You are all the aunts' and uncles' firstborn nephew.
Jonathan, you are our gift from God.
Thank you, dear Jesus for
his talents and special gifts,
his precious face,
his sparkle,
his winning smile,
his kindness,
his special personality,
his love for You,
his desire to see souls saved,
his service for You with music,
his special walk,
his physically fit, lean body,
his athletic ability,
his fun-loving, teasing nature,
his desire to eat healthily,
his loyalty,
his uncomplaining spirit,
his positive nature,
his desire to help others,
his strong work ethic, regardless of pay,
his tenacity,
his strength of purpose.

January 18, 2000

Jonathan's birthday arrives. He is twenty-one years old and still in the hospital.

Morning Minutes

Despite my inner anxiety due to Jonathan's illness, I am again reminded of the song "How Can I Fear" that was written for Jonathan when he was young.

I don't have to fear tomorrow because God is already there.

The antidote for fear is faith. If you were to take out all the stories about men and women of God in the Bible, who had to trust God despite unbelievable circumstances, you'd only have a few pages left.

I journal:

> *Dear Lord, I will surrender every cell, every fiber, every brain wave to You. If I lived back in the days of Noah or Abraham, I wonder . . . would my faith be strong enough to be recorded in the Bible?*

I have a missionary friend who the previous year had asked me to give her son a twenty-first birthday party at our home. In their family, twenty-first birthdays are so special. As she is on the mission field, she is unable to give him the celebration. I am happy to do it, although our own son is very ill at the time.

Now a year later, it's Jonathan's turn to have his twenty-first birthday. It is devastating to celebrate in a mental hospital scenario, but celebrate we do. In the hospital, you can only have a couple of visitors at a time. Somehow the staff allows us to have a birthday party in the lobby of the lockdown unit, complete with cake and presents. My parents and our other children are allowed to come.

I remember after the party is over and our family is gone, the head nurse of the unit takes Ron and me to a back room and shows us a documentary film on schizophrenia. One nurse begs her not to do this; it is not the right time. The head nurse goes ahead, telling us we need to accept the fact that Jonathan's illness is close to behaving like schizophrenia. Watching the film is gut-wrenching. It is beyond overwhelming to think that this is our son's fate.

The documentary we watch is about a set of identical twin boys who both suddenly become schizophrenic, within a day apart from each other. The first twin comes home from working at Blockbuster™, puts his head down between his hands on the kitchen table and tells his mom that something is very wrong in his head.

The very next day, the second twin dittos the first. Although medicines help these men to function, schizophrenia becomes part of their lives. The film shows both men in their present adult years. It is apparent that the two men struggle, but both are able to work part time.

I am not ready for this unveiling. We have just celebrated Jonathan's birthday in a lockdown unit and are now told something akin to schizophrenia is Jonathan's future. Happy birthday?

It is in this facility that Jonathan's diagnosis goes from bipolar, a lesser evil, to schizoaffective, an illness somewhere in the realm between bipolar and schizophrenia. The doctors at Charter tell Ron and me that Jonathan, with youth and intelligence on his side, has a 30% chance of improvement. We cling to this hope.

While at Charter, I attend some helpful classes with Jonathan. In one class we learn the difference between alcohol and psychiatric medicines. Some sufferers, like my Uncle Elmer, self-medicate with alcohol. Those who take the psychiatric medicines feel better while taking them but come back to base "O" when the medicine is out of their system. Those living with mental illness who turn to alcohol to feel better end up feeling worse when the alcohol is out of their system. They now have a dual problem—mental illness and alcoholism. I am so grateful Jonathan never resorts to alcohol.

January 21, 2000

Morning Minutes

I feel like my spiritual muscles are being strengthened by the resistance I am getting from lifting the heavy weights God is placing in my incorporeal gym. When a bodybuilder lifts weights, the muscles are first broken down before they can rejuvenate and build up. This is what trials must be doing to my spiritual muscles.

Sarah shares with me one of her favorite Scripture passages: "Blessed be the Lord my strength which teacheth my hands to war, and my fingers to fight: my goodness, and my fortress; my high tower, and my deliverer; my shield, and he in whom I trust" (Psalm 144:1–2).

One of my favorite Scriptures is Joshua 1:9. "Have not I commanded thee? Be strong and of a good courage; be not afraid, neither be thou dismayed: for the Lord thy God is with thee whithersoever thou goest."

Finally, on Friday, January 21, we receive a call from Charter Hospital that Jon is improved enough to come home. What a day of rejoicing this is. The following day, Saturday, January 22, it starts snowing in Greenville. Because of this, all Sunday church services are canceled due to the weather. I'll never forget it. Sunday is January 23 and my forty-sixth birthday. What a happy day. I get to enjoy all of my family at our home, surrounded by beautiful snow.

Jon has improved in the hospital. He takes his medicine, smiles, eats, and talks a little more. Jon is now on what is called a "cocktail" of four meds:

Haldol—an antipsychotic for delusional thinking,

Neurontin—a mood stabilizer,

Effexor—an antidepressant, and

Cogentin—to lessen his chances of getting Tardive Dyskinesia from the antipsychotic. (TD, as it is called, is an irreversible side effect from antipsychotics, causing involuntary muscle movements in the tongue or face.)

Dave Pennington has told us that after finding the right medicine(s), it takes about two months for the fog to lift. The Haldol that Jon is taking is referred to as a medicinal straight jacket. Haldol is often administered by injection when a mental illness sufferer needs sedation, such as when acting violently after being picked up by the police. The medicine is so hard core that it causes Jon to walk like an old man while taking it. One of Jonathan's friends tells him that while on Haldol, he felt like he had marbles in his mouth while trying to speak.

After Jon's release from Charter, I remember taking him to a music concert some of his former classmates are attending. Several of them come up to talk to Jonathan. When he tries to answer their questions, his brain short circuits. He speaks in spurts interrupted by short blips of silence. This is a common occurrence now. I can ask Jon a question like, "Do you want ketchup on your hamburger?" He doesn't answer immediately. By the time he says, "Yes," I have forgotten what I asked.

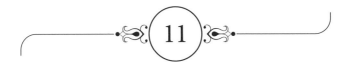

Living with Mental Illness

February 1, 2000

Our journey of mental illness with our son lives on.

In order to understand more about the mental illness with which our son is dealing, I have researched its history and measurements. One thing I read over and over—if any part of the human brain is missing or broken, functioning at 100% is not possible.

Studies suggest that most doctors today want to qualify mental illness as organic to strengthen their belief that it is physically based. Some doctors still exist, however, who believe it is not. Fortunately, their numbers are few.

I want to emphasize again that I am in no way a mental health professional. I hope not to sound like I think I am. My experience is instead a 24/7, hands on, multiple-doctor-visits, hours-of-reading, listening-to-hundreds-of-testimonies one. If you, on the other hand, are not familiar with mental health issues, it would be helpful for you to learn a little about the illness to more fully understand Jonathan's story. The following quotations are taken from *Diagnostic and Statistical Manual of Mental Disorders*, Fifth Edition: DSM-5, updated August 28, 2020.

Mental illness diagnoses criteria are:

1. ***Bipolar***—average age of onset, 18 years old

   - "a complex mental health condition characterized by severe shifts in mood accompanied by changes in energy and activity levels. The condition affects an individual's mood, thoughts, and behaviors." Bipolar usually has lifts back to periods of almost (95%) normalcy; the more episodes an individual has, the worse the long-term prognosis and the lower the percentage of normalcy restored; multiple episodes cause the dying of brain cells and the decision making and emotional state of "normal periods" to be compromised.

   - *Mania* exhibits "a distinct period of abnormally and persistently elevated, expansive, or irritable mood, lasting at least one week." Sometimes a person in mania believes God is speaking directly to them, often telling them to do troublesome actions. There is an increase in energy and activity levels; over-the-top buying sprees and hoarding; not sleeping but still feeling on top of the world; over-the-top romantic ideation; pressured speech—continuous talking, often rapid and excitable; reckless driving; violent agitation; mania almost always ending in depression—thus the term bipolar, incorporating the law of gravity—what goes up, must come down

   - *Depression* exhibits "two main criteria: depressed mood and anhedonia. A depressed mood has to do with sadness or negative emotions. Anhedonia means that you no longer feel any pleasure or interest in the things you once enjoyed." A depressed person has feelings of being in a dark hole that leaves them unable to see to the top. They have slowed thinking and movements; impaired concentration; lack of motivation; sleeping too much or too little; isolation; no facial expression; catatonic states; crying spells for no apparent reason; suicidal thoughts

- some people dealing with bipolar, never exhibit mania but only deal with depression

2. *Major Depressive Disorder*—average age of onset, 27 years old

- a mood disorder—exhibits depression symptoms only

- there are six symptoms of depression that begin with an "A"—asthenia (muscle weakness and flu-like symptoms), apathy (not caring), amotivation (no motivation), anergia (low or no energy), alogia (not talking), and anhedonia (no feeling of pleasure)

3. *Schizophrenia*—average age of onset, late teens to early 20s for men and late 20s to early 30s for women

- "a serious psychiatric disorder. It is characterized by a combination of 'positive,' 'negative,' and cognitive symptoms. These symptoms are chronic and usually appear in early adulthood."

- a thought disorder that is constant—has no lifts back to normalcy as does bipolar, "including difficulty forming cohesive thoughts, thought blocking, and rapidly changing thoughts."

- has positive symptoms such as: "hallucinations of seeing, hearing, or smelling things that are not there;" delusions—"a strong belief in ideas that are not grounded in reality and holding onto them even when evidence is presented that proves it wrong;" paranoia—"fearful of things that are not really there; hearing voices in which are derogatory or threatening"

- has negative symptoms such as: blunting of affect—no facial expressions, poverty of speech and thought, apathy, reduced social drive, loss of motivation

- the majority of schizophrenics will usually experience both depressive and manic symptoms, extreme agitation, and obsessive-compulsive actions

- can develop unusual movements consisting "of repetitive movements or lengthy episodes of being very still (catatonic) and unusually slow movements."

- high anxiety sometimes including panic attacks

Schizoaffective Disorder lies somewhere between bipolar and schizophrenia—probably more like schizophrenia with no lifts back to normalcy without medicinal intervention. It has "characterization with both psychotic and mood symptom, either concurrently or at different points."

Schizophrenia is not a split personality as some have been led to believe. A split personality disorder is referred as *Multiple Personality Disorder*—"a dissociative condition that is difficult to understand, diagnose, treat and discuss."

There are other mental disorders as well. *Anxiety Disorder and Obsessive-Compulsive Disorder* are two we mentioned that often show symptoms in bipolar, depression, and mania. There are also many more auxiliary diagnoses that we do not have time or space to discuss in this book.

The earliest mention of mental illness was by Hippocrates, known as "the father of medicine" (c. 460 BC–c. 370 BC). He categorized extreme lows by what we now call "depression" and extreme highs by what we call "mania." Hippocrates' theory was that melancholia was caused by black bile in the human system and mania by too much yellow bile. Aretaeus, a Greek physician in the first century, was the first to recognize that the two extreme moods originated with a problem in the brain.

In 1851, French psychiatrist Jean-Pierre Faret, incorporated a term to describe what we know today as bipolar—one extreme mood disorder cycling to the other. He called it "la folie circulaire" or "circular insanity."

Sedatives were the only medicines found in the 1800s to inhibit the irrational behaviors on both ends of the spectrum—sedatives such as alkaloids, bromides, and barbiturates. Eventually, a man named John Cade pioneered helping those with extreme highs and lows by experimenting with and finding the successes of lithium.

In the early 1900s, German psychiatrist Emil Kraepelin observed that some mental illness had intervals of normalcy, thus separating it from schizophrenia. Kraepelin coined the term "manic–depressive illness" describing those who flip-flopped between mania and depression.

In 1955, there was estimated to be 560,000 living with mental illness in the United States alone. By then there was a revolution of psychopharmaceutical drugs, discovered accidentally when anti-epileptic medications were administered that also helped manic–depressive symptoms.

President John Kennedy, encouraged by the new drug finds, thought it more humane to treat the mentally ill with medicine on an outpatient basis than to lock them up in mental institutions. In 1963 Kennedy signed legislation giving grants to community mental health support systems to take the place of the former mental institutions.

The idea was good, but the eventual shutting down of mental institutions was not. Far too many facilities were closed, leading to the shortage of beds we still have today. In 1980, President Jimmy Carter signed into law The Mental Health Systems Act, giving large sums of money to facilitate the community centers. Also, in the 1980s, the term *manic–depressive* was changed to *bipolar*.

The very next year in 1981, when President Ronald Reagan came into office, he revoked most of President Carter's legislation and funding. The patient's bill of rights was a section of the bill that was not repealed. The problem with the patient's bill of rights that remained in effect is that it doesn't give any rights to the caregivers. The rights of the mentally ill exceed the rights of the caregivers, making it very difficult to get a loved one in desperate need into a hospital. The one with mental illness, who is not living in reality, creating trauma in your home, and refusing to take medication, can only be institutionalized if you can prove they are a harm to themselves or you. What good comes from waiting to that point?

A mentally ill person may have threatened harm to oneself just days before, and you may even have it documented in something like a text, but if the one in a mental episode does not repeat the threat to the police when they arrive, they are not allowed under law to take the affected individual to a place of safety.

The one with the mental breakdown is unaware of his state of mind and yet is allowed to stay in the home where other inhabitants are traumatized due to bizarre behaviors and temper rages. Many mentally ill are cast out of their homes as a result. This is part of the reason so many mentally ill remain homeless on our streets. Senseless!

The new medications found to address these disorders have not accomplished everything that was hoped in 1963. Some severe mental illnesses have not been helped at all by the medications. Due to the closing of institutions, there is a lack of adequate beds and consequently, people committed to institutions are usually only kept for a few days.

As we now know, it takes much longer to find the right medicine treatment. The shortage of beds we see has caused the price of institutionalization to skyrocket—another reason many with mental health issues end up on our streets, in our prisons, and in our homes.

(Taking a brief peek forward to February 23, 2018—President Donald Trump is recorded to proclaim the reopening of mental institutions. Will we see this come to pass?)

February 26, 2000

I journal:

> *Ben [Farrell] goes to Disney World with his family in January and brings back a pretty silver necklace for Tara with a "T" on it. Alyssa performs in a piano competition held at Furman University. We find out she has made it into the finals. Good things again amidst the bad.*

Although Jon has continued mental struggles, he remains a sweetheart when he is on his medications, which is a blessing. He is presently on a winning combination and is so kind to each of our family members. He plays with Jason who is now seven years old. Jon likes to spoil me—rubs my back, hugs me, and tells me often that he loves me.

Jonathan remains very quiet, not initiating much conversation. Ben Farrell, Josh Rohrer, and Eleazer Yanson come home with our family one Sunday for lunch. The three boys play ping pong, and I hear Jonathan let out one of his deep belly laughs for the first time in months. What a beautiful sound it is.

Neuroleptics, medicines for mental health disorders, many times have adverse side effects. This is unfortunate for the sufferer! In order for the brain chemicals to improve, the body is going to experience negative "this and thats." Among some of the possible side effects are weight gain, especially frontal; constant cravings for carbohydrates; hair loss; extreme fatigue; fuzzy thoughts; akathisia (restless leg syndrome all over the body), and/or Tardive Dyskinesia.

It's a win/lose situation. You win because you can again function; you lose because of the drastic side effects. In the end, functioning trumps.

The doctors at Charter have encouraged Ron and me to keep a daily evaluation on Jonathan's symptoms. 5 is good and 1 is not so good. On page 85 is a sample of one of our many journaling entries we make of Jonathan's symptoms.

Emotions are interesting phenomena. All human beings have them because God included them as part of our biological makeups. Many studies are presently being done on the hundreds of brain chemicals that create each emotion: anxiety, sadness, anger, joy, fear, and so on. I asked my Uncle Vic, Dad's youngest brother who is a psychologist, how he explained emotions and their disturbances.

Uncle Vic explained them to me with a graph of emotions and moods (see page 86). If you go from 1% to 100%, most of our emotions fall into a range from 40% to 60%. Right in the middle is 50%, the midway norm. Going from 50% up to 60% are where very motivated, driven, and fast-paced people live. Going from 50% down to 40% is where laid-back, calm, and slow-moving people live.

Biblical counseling is important to help one remember the truths of Scripture and God is good, even through illness.

95 possible points

"If you abide in Me, and My words abide in you,
ask whatever you wish,
and it shall be done for you." John 15

	2/6	7	8	9	10	11	12	13	14	15	16	17	18	19	20
Eating Amount/appetite	4/3	4/3	4/3	4/3	5/3	3/3	3/3	4/4	5/4	5/4	3/3	5/3	4/2	4/2	4/2
Sleeping	3	3	4	4	3	4		5	5	4	2	5	3	3	4+
Hygiene	5	5	5	5	5	5	5	5	5	5	3	5	5	5	5
Affect: Smiling	5		4	5	5	4	4	4	4	3	3	4	3	3	5
Emotion	2	2	2	2+	4	3	4	3	4	3	3	4	2	2	3
Eyes	2	2	3	2	3	2	2	2	3	2	2	3	2	2	3
Socializing	3+	3	3	4+	5	2	2	5	5	3	4	4	2	3	4
Concentrate	3	3	3	3+	4	3	3	4	4	3	4	4	3	3	4
Calm	5	5	5	5	5	5	5	5	5	4	4	4+	4	4	5
Cognitive-thought block "all-there" delusional	3 2	3 2	4 2	4 2	4 2	4 2	4 2	5 2	4 3	5 3	4 5	4 4	4 3	4 3	4+ 3
sweet	4	5	5	5	5	5	5	5	5	5	5	4	4	4	5
Work/chores	5	5	5	5	5	5	5	5	5	5	1	5	5	5	5
Communicate	1	1	1	3	4	2	3	4	4	4	3	4	3	3	5
Pacing	4	4	3	4	4	5	5	5	5	5	3	4	4	4	4
Music	2	2	2	2	2	2	3	3	3	3	4	3	3	4	
Home.. Initiative	2	2	2	2	3	2	3	3	3	2	4	3	3	3	
Humor/teasing	1	1	1	3	3	2	1	2	3	2	2	4	3	3	3
	64	60	66	69	76	60	63	74	80	70	55	79	63	63	75
	S	M	T	W	Th			Sun		M					Sun

Sample Journal Page

Mood Grid—Manic/depressive-disorder of the moods

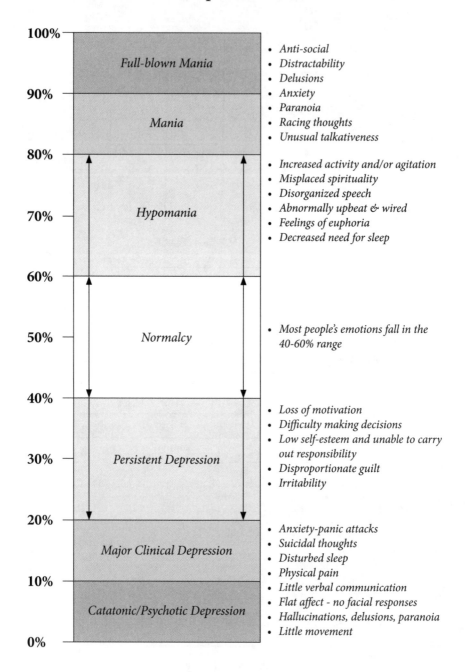

100%	Full-blown Mania	• Anti-social • Distractability • Delusions
90%	Mania	• Anxiety • Paranoia • Racing thoughts • Unusual talkativeness
80%	Hypomania	• Increased activity and/or agitation • Misplaced spirituality • Disorganized speech • Abnormally upbeat & wired • Feelings of euphoria • Decreased need for sleep
60%		
50%	Normalcy	• Most people's emotions fall in the 40-60% range
40%		
30%	Persistent Depression	• Loss of motivation • Difficulty making decisions • Low self-esteem and unable to carry out responsibility • Disproportionate guilt • Irritability
20%	Major Clinical Depression	• Anxiety-panic attacks • Suicidal thoughts • Disturbed sleep • Physical pain
10%	Catatonic/Psychotic Depression	• Little verbal communication • Flat affect - no facial responses • Hallucinations, delusions, paranoia • Little movement
0%		

Most all of us experience highs and lows, but usually stay within the 40 to 60% range.

When you start going above 60% on the graph, you gradually ascend into a manic direction. At some point, you are in full-blown mania—not sleeping, but feeling euphoric; superficially close to God; trouble focusing; pressured speech; and so forth. Mania is like a fast-moving train. If you do not put the brakes on, the train accelerates faster and faster.

When you start going below 40% on the graph, you gradually start descending into a depressive direction. At some point, you are in full-blown clinical depression—unable to pull yourself up by your own bootstraps; unable to get out of bed; having no facial expressions; feeling no euphoric emotions; and stopping communication, eating, and interacting socially.

Depression in its severest form can get a person to the point of a catatonic state. Depression is like a train that has traveled into a tunnel and stopped. You sit in the darkness without the hope of the train ever moving again into the light.

May 2000

Jonathan is now mentally doing only so-so. The meds obviously need adjustment. Most of 2000 is kind of a blur. What I do remember is our dear friends, Senator Dave Thomas and his wife Fran, coming to our support. Every fall, a tradition is for our two families go apple picking, complete with a tailgate picnic.

One of these times after Jon's illness has begun, Dave asks Jonathan to say the blessing before we eat. All Jonathan can get out is, "Dear Lord" before his brain chemicals short circuit. Ron soon comes to his rescue and finishes the prayer. David has no idea what Jonathan can and cannot do.

December 26, 2000

I journal:

> *Be patient. Trust God. Let the joy of the Lord be your strength.*
> *God, please help us. And carry us. God is Almighty. He is love.*
> *He is mercy.*

Mental illness is a worldwide problem.

- Nearly one in five U.S adults live with a mental illness (51.5 million in 2019).[7]

- When it comes to countries, India is the most depressed country in the world, according to the World Health Organization, followed by China and the USA. India, China and the US are the most affected countries by anxiety, schizophrenia and bipolar disorder, according to WHO.[8]

Very unfortunately, history substantiates that many suffering from mental illness were kept separate from society. Particularly ill-fated were those killed by droves in German concentration camps. Existing still today: abortion is mandatory in China for those whose heritage includes mental illness. Interestingly, my family would not be here today if we had lived in Germany or China.

---

[7] https://www.nimh.nih.gov/health/statistics/mental-illness
[8] https://www.indiatoday.in/education-today/gk-current-affairs/story/india-is-the-most-depressed-country-in-the-world-mental-health-day-2018–1360096–2018–10–10

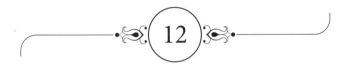

A Roller Coaster Ride

January 2001

We are now entering year three of Jonathan's illness. Jonathan is twenty-two, Tara-twenty, Alyssa-eighteen, Megan-twelve, and Jason-eight.

Morning Minutes

Every morning I determine to predisposition my heart and mind to prepare myself—in case a rough day is ahead or if I am to receive bad news. Although it has taken a while into Jonathan's illness, I am finally able to pray: "Lord, I am ready for battle— bring it on! Jon needs to see courage in me. The ball is in your court, Lord."

When I am overwhelmed, lead me to the Rock that is higher than I. (Psalms 61:2 paraphrased)

The first years into Jonathan's illness, Ron and I rarely talk about his situation to others. We continue leading the music program faithfully at Calvary every Sunday and Wednesday night. Jonathan comes to church on the Sundays that he feels able to handle facing people. Sometimes he even sings in the choir.

Since the onset of Jonathan's illness, his solo-singing days are over. At the beginning, he on occasion sings in some special groups, staring at his shoelaces the entire song. People from time to time come up and say, "What's going on with Jonathan?" We really feel uncomfortable sharing his illness. Knowing what to say is difficult. We try to briefly explain the best that we can without giving too much detail. It seems better for our son, at the beginning, to keep his illness to ourselves. We also continue writing, producing, and running Majesty Music, although we never leave Jonathan alone at our home. Someone is always with him 24/7.

For us, our son living with mental illness can be compared to going on an extreme roller coaster ride.

You go up and down; up and down.
You jerk to the left and suddenly to the right when you least expect it.
You look over the edge and cannot see land or water.
You feel completely helpless.
Your heart sinks to your stomach.
You ain't controlin' nothin'.

The roller coaster onlooker tries to understand how it feels for the mental illness rider but cannot. The onlooker can see what is happening from the outside but is unable to experience it from within. While a mental sufferer is tossed to and fro, screaming on the roller coaster life experience, *you* are only the observer. (Caregivers, however, are seated very close behind.)

When an individual is suffering from mental illness, one must be careful not to say the wrong thing. Heaven forbid you become the one to push the sufferer over the edge into the abyss. My Aunt Eunice, Dad's older sister who dealt with schizophrenia for sixty-five years, said that until you have been in clinical depression yourself, along with the paranoia of schizophrenia, you cannot begin to imagine the mental inferno that is experienced.

I want to mention here that not all those who deal with mental health issues are alike. This is because of the different types of personalities and levels of spirituality of the people affected. The illness is as individual as the individuals who have it.

Mental disorders also have different degrees of severity as with any illness—from mild, to moderate, to severe. Some live normal, productive lives. Some live normally at times and tumultuously at other times. Some live tumultuously all the time. Most all those whose mental illness impedes their ability to function must stay faithful to their medicine(s).

My Aunt Eunice had three children, one of whom continues to suffer with a mental disorder. I asked Aunt Eunice once which is worse, suffering with the disease yourself or watching your child suffer with it. Her answer was, "There is no contest." I thought to myself, *She's going to say watching your child.* She instead continued, "Having it yourself is the worst. You cannot think clearly. You are afraid to talk to anyone. You feel like you are at the bottom of a hole with no hope of climbing out."

Let me be explicit: living with someone who has severe mental illness is challenging for the sufferer as well as the caregiver. The disease taxes both to their extreme emotional limits. Continuous mental stress is unimaginable until you have experienced it for yourself or for a loved one. Aunt Eunice's response helps me understand in just a small way what my Jonathan is going through.

Watching my son suffer—becoming anti-social, quiet, catatonic, and delusional—is horrible. It is like a death—death of the son we once knew. During the course of some illnesses, you hurt for your child, but you can still communicate with them. Mental illness, on the other hand, often takes your child away from you. They cannot reason their way back and, when ill, become a different person.

The first years of Jon's illness are exhausting for him, leaving him much of the time in bed, flat on his back, and staring at the ceiling—sometimes beating his head against the wall and sometimes ripping his clothes into shreds. Trying to find the right medicine or medicine combo for mental illness has been and continues to be extremely challenging. When it is not correct, an already bad situation is made worse.

A typical scenario, unfortunately, is when someone finds a good medicine or combination thereof, they begin to feel better and so eventually decide to take themselves off. This is due to not wanting to be on medicine permanently and disliking the prominent side effects. The person suffering usually chooses not to take their medication(s) without telling anyone in order to skip the drama. Do we really blame them?

January 9, 2001

I journal:

> *But he knoweth the way that I take: when he hath tried me, I shall come forth as gold. (Job 23:10)*
>
> *Jon continues to have bizarre eating habits. They are like rituals. Ron takes our family to Atlanta over the weekend. Jon does okay. He takes all his own food with him. Misses his medicine on Sunday. Pretty troubled by the evening.*

We try to figure out what is going on in Jonathan's brain, but cannot. Our brains are mysteries.

Due to study and advances in psychopharmacology, neuroscience, and genetics, our psychiatrists now have a better biological understanding of the brain rather than the outdated psychoanalysis they used to employ.

Our brains have numerous chemicals, or neurotransmitters, that serve as electrical currents, jumping from synapse to synapse, allowing us to think and function. "Brain chemicals, called neurotransmitters, are packaged in tiny, bubble-like compartments known as vesicles. [Images we have] show vesicles at the end of one brain cell that are ready to cross a small gap into another brain cell . . . billions of brain cells called neurons transmit signals to each other. . . . It is an extremely fast and efficient process—one central to everything the brain does, including learning, memorizing, planning, reasoning, and enabling movement."[9].

As I have mentioned, some individuals have more of the brain chemical called serotonin, causing them to naturally be driven and passionate. Some have less serotonin, causing them to be laid back and calm. Some have more of the anxiety chemical causing them to be fearful and anxious. The list continues.

"The brain is the most complex organ in the human body. It produces our every thought, action, memory, feeling and experience of the world. This jelly-like mass of tissue, weighing in at around 1.4 kilograms, contains a staggering one hundred billion nerve cells, or neurons."[10]

For the average adult in a resting state, the brain consumes about 20 percent of the body's energy. Though scientific research into the brain is growing at an astronomical rate, we still know relatively little about how it actually functions and what causes brain abnormalities.

The human brain is phenomenal, allowing Handel to write the Messiah in just three short weeks. My Down's Syndrome nephew Jordan has memorized the page number and song name of every Ron Hamilton song in the *Majesty Hymnal*. How is this possible? We cannot fully understand the intricacies of the brain God created.

As with any other organ of the body, something can go wrong with our brains and/or our brain chemicals, causing emotional and/or thinking problems. Suffice it to say for now, and for me to repeat, that mental illness is a very real physical and organic illness.

A study done by Andreasen's team discovered that those affected with schizophrenia suffered the most brain tissue loss in the first two years of the illness, but then the damage curiously plateaued[11]. MRIs also

---

[9]https://www.brainfacts.org/archives/2011/neurotransmitters-how-brain-cells-use-chemicals-to-communicate
[10]https://www.newscientist.com/article/dn9969-introduction-the-human-brain

showed schizophrenia sufferers have less healthy brain tissue, although many are intelligent, even before the first symptoms present. Although study is still being done presently, much more research is needed.

Incidentally, one should note the striking similarities between the causes of epilepsy and mental illness. Epilepsy is an abnormal brain activity resulting from genetics, trauma, or injury to the head, medical conditions that affect the brain, developmental disorders, or infectious illness to name just a few. "The two [epilepsy and mental illness] can occur together and be caused by the same thing. For example, low oxygen, injury or infection at birth may cause mental retardation, epilepsy, and cerebral palsy"[12].

Mental illness does not always involve psychosis. In fact, most mental illnesses do not. People in psychosis can do bizarre things such as removing their clothes in public (or on a commercial air flight as happened to one of my acquaintances), curling up in a fetal position for hours and days, screaming on the side of a highway at passersby, and many more peculiar behaviors.

Psychosis comes down to the fact that when a person is severely mentally impaired, they simply cannot think rationally. The sufferer slips from the grasp of reality, and his behaviors follow suit. To a normally functioning individual, psychotic actions seem "crazy." To the mentally ill, however, their behaviors seem perfectly normal.

Hence rationalizing with a person who is in psychosis is most often futile. His thoughts, called "circular reasoning," go round and round. The counselor no sooner thinks they are getting somewhere, when the counselee ends up back to step one. Actually, persons in psychosis believe that everyone else around them is ill but not them.

January 18, 2001

It is Jonathan's twenty-second birthday. My journal continued:

---

[11]https://www.brainfacts.org/brain-anatomy-and-function/anatomy/2019/how-much-energy-does-the-brain-use-020119

[12]https://www.epilepsy.com/article/2016/11/epilepsy-and-psychological-disorders

We are still in a fix with Jonathan. He sleeps all day, talks to no one, and eats some in the night. What he eats is more normal. Is not doing compulsive acts. Is very withdrawn. I am so frustrated but trying to rest in the peace that God is in control. I have never faced anything so painful in my entire life. I love you, Lord . . . and I love you, Jonathan. I can hardly wait until heaven. Jonathan will be all right, and all my pain will be gone.

February 1, 2001

Morning Minutes

When we suffer, we partake of His glory.
God chooses whom He allows to suffer.
Each time we suffer, a little bit of glory is sent up to heaven
that we'll enjoy for all eternity.

Depakote is added to Jonathan's meds to no benefit. Determining the correct medicines for mental disorders is not only difficult for the doctor but a strain on the entire family. The more serious the disorder, the greater the trauma and time it takes to find the right medicinal elixir.

Marriages and siblings are all affected by the family member suffering. When the illness becomes episodic or continuous, household members can be taxed to their extreme limits. I must conclude, however, that our family becomes very tight-knit as we all trust God together. Pain draws us closer to the cross and to each other.

Ron, desperate to get help for Jonathan, calls the Greenville Rescue Mission. Mr. Slocum later writes us this note:

I was the Director of the Greenville Rescue Mission for many years. Ron called me one day asking about what we might be able to do to help Jonathan. "Would either the Mission or the Overcomers possibly be a help?"

He and Jonathan came to the Mission for a talk. I remember we met in the parking lot behind the building. Jonathan was not willing to get out but was willing to talk with me. I remember squatting down for quite a while talking. He did let me pray for him but didn't want the Overcomers or the Mission. I remember observing his confusion. I know I prayed for him for quite a while. I have always wondered if we could have been some help.

—William Slocum

Well documented are that traumatic events can trigger serious depression in an individual, but when the trauma eases, the depression usually lifts as well. In this scenario, the depression often lets up sometime after the trigger is gone. In contrast, mental illnesses can be triggered by trauma, antibiotics, and drugs; however, when the trigger has passed, most often the illness does not. Also, mental illness caused by biological malfunctions of the brain do not necessarily need a trigger.

Some individuals experience a level of depression from other exterior circumstances—circumstances such as not having meaningful connections at home, attending college yet unsure of vocation, or even unhappiness in the workplace. One of Jon's school friends, Will Gray, has a passion to reach into the community and help people connect at work. I ran into Will at a coffee house recently and felt like the meeting was a God thing. Will called it *Spirit-dipity*. I asked him to explain his ministry, thinking it might be a help to a reader who is experiencing a loss of meaning and/or purpose in their work. Will writes:

Over the last decade, I've had the privilege of serving as a vocational guide to dozens and dozens of people who felt lost in their work life. Some were experiencing a classic mid-life crisis. Others were teens who felt puzzled about what to study in college, and still others were struggling with how to translate themselves and their gifts into a version of retirement that included more than golf!

Most of those clients were frustrated and sad; many were in the undertow of depression as well, convinced there was something wrong with them.

Along the way, I've learned what Gallup has learned: 87% of workers worldwide are emotionally disengaged from their work, which means that only 13% have found what we might call "what they were made to do." Yes, the statistics are better in North America, but not by much. Here it is estimated that 29% are engaged, which means two out of every three working adults still show up to work feeling a little like a zombie and not much like an image-bearer who's flourishing where they're planted.

Feeling disconnected from your purpose is only one of many lost connections we can experience in life. The loss is powerful, however, in a world where we're often overly defined by what we do. One of the most common questions you get when you meet someone new is, "What do you do?" Even if you don't like your answer, you're going to be repeating it a lot.

We're made uniquely, that's for certain. The journey to discover and understand our "madeness" (and what it means for our work life) is often a journey we don't even know can be made. And so the path lies unwalked, our disconnection lingers, and the voices in our head keep telling us that we are in this situation because we don't matter after all. They are lies, of course, but sometimes they feel painfully true.

—Will Gray, Founder, www.vocationality.com

Of course, for the Christian, the purpose of life is to glorify God. Very unfortunate are the many who never discover this divine purpose. Since a majority of our lives tend to be in the workplace, however, one must come to a grappling point that what they are doing is meaningful and purposeful—for the saved and unsaved alike. Depression can result if the issue is not resolved.

Biblical counseling and the reading of Scripture is essential for a person to find purpose in God. Meeting with someone like Will is beneficial for someone who wants to find work that is meaningful. Actually, Will has been able to use his ministry to lead people to find God and accept Jesus into their hearts.

Ron and I have been told many times by numerous doctors that what Jonathan is experiencing is a serious, debilitating mental illness. We have daily, sometimes minute by minute discussions on what we should do next regarding Jon's situation and symptoms. The discussions are without emotion on Ron's side and passionate on mine. Will there ever be relief?

Faith on Autopilot

April 1, 2001

Morning Minutes

Faith, mighty faith, The promises it sees;
It looks to God alone, Laughs at impossibilities,
And cries, "It shall be done."

My faith is on autopilot.

Ron and I hear about a good alternative doctor who runs myriads of tests on his patients. He is located not far away in Columbia, South Carolina, so we decide to give him a try. After all the tests come back, the doctor puts Jonathan on over a hundred vitamin and herb supplements—none of which he is ever willing to take. Finally, Jon agrees to take only one pill a day. Ron and I are convinced that the "one pill" should be the doctor's recommended medicine.

I wish we had started with this doctor.

Going through mental illness is like the soldier who wore Confederate pants and a Union jacket; he got shot at both ends. The illness shoots you at one end and some friends at the other.

Let me stress the importance of being a support to anyone you know who is dealing with mental health issues. Ron and I never felt like we were judgmental before Jonathan's journey. As caregivers of a child, very dear to our hearts, who is enduring a serious mental illness, however—we are now even less so. Our empathy for those who suffer in any fashion could not be greater.

How do you help a family who has a loved one or friend who is living with mental illness and is unable to function outside of the home? You can help by:

- opening up your arms and heart to them.

- committing to continual prayer for them.

- supporting the caregivers with love and kindness.

- letting the person with mental illness know you love them by note or gift, via the caregiver if necessary. Just tell them you miss seeing them and maybe share something going on in your life. (Someone with mental illness does not like to be confronted about their illness and more than likely not be open to an in-home visit.)

- texting the person with mental illness, if you are a close friend, to see if they would like to go for a drive, a walk, or out to eat. Don't be offended if they are not open to your reaching out. Gently try again later.

- not criticizing the family to others or speaking ill about them behind their back.

- respecting the person with mental illness, as well as the entire family, and not judging them.

- destigmatizing mental illness by treating it like other illnesses.

- treating the mentally ill person no differently than you treat others.

We, as Christians, should be better than anyone else in the way we accept and treat others. Let's set the standard.

April 30, 2001

I journal:

> *There is a specific purpose in each of our individual lives. You give us everything we need to accomplish that purpose. We each have a way that we bring honor to You, Lord. Dear Jesus, I refuse to think any negative thoughts. Lord, I want to be totally conformed to your image. I want my thoughts to be Your thoughts. That is what You want. And that is what I want. Doubt is the dark room the devil takes you into to get your negatives developed.*

The negative belongs to the enemy. I have to discipline the flabby muscles of my mind by exercising them. I don't dare let even a single hair fall over to that side—thoughts taken from Galatians 5:22–26 and Ephesians 6:16.

Ron and I read about a bipolar specialist at Johns Hopkins Hospital in Baltimore, Maryland. We decide to take Jonathan to him for an evaluation. His name is Dr. Francis Mondimore, MD. After interviewing Jonathan, this doctor gives him a diagnosis of major depressive disorder with psychotic features. Dr. Mondimore is very kind, listens, and gives us good advice. He believes our best hope medically is to "hang in there" and keep experimenting with different medicines.

Our faith remains on autopilot.

You are seeing by now what a rat race it can be to find the right medicine(s) to help with chronic mental illness. Many times, you get a diagnosis only after a medicine is found that helps. If a mood stabilizer helps—bipolar; an antipsychotic—schizophrenia; an antidepressant—major depressive disorder. The list goes on.

I have a friend who has a loved one with some type of mental disorder. The family is in the throes right now as I write in 2020 of finding the right medicine(s). Their doctor tells them the only way to get a definitive diagnosis is by autopsy. Will we even care at that point?

May 2001

Morning Minutes

The book of Psalms from the Bible becomes the mainstay of my devotional time. Our friend and counselor Dave Pennington tells me he marks verses of promise with an anchor beside it.

I do the same.

The book of Psalms has anchors drawn all over its pages with Jon's initials and the date that I mark it. I can almost catalog my faith journey through Jonathan's illness by the anchored verses and dates.

Back home in Greenville, I ask Ron if we should look into shock treatment for our son. My Aunt Eunice and my Grandma Fox have had success from shock treatment for their depression. I convince Ron for us to take Jon to the only doctor at the time in our area who does shock therapy. This doctor tells us that Jonathan is definitely a candidate for it, but he would hold off if at all possible and try more medicines first. Another dead-end street.

Faith is on autopilot.

We learn from this doctor that shock treatments are popular and successful for some with mental illness. Many patients will set up an appointment for their annual treatment. By far the preferred route of treatment for mental illness, however, is psychotherapeutic medication.

As before-mentioned: a break-through discovery occurred when physicians found that medicines for epilepsy helped treat bipolar. How could medicine treat symptoms if depression and mania were not a physical problem? More pointedly, how can these treatments have a clear, predictable result in returning a person to a normative and functional mental state, if the problem doesn't lie in brain chemistry?

When you have a mental illness, stay on the medication(s) that are found to help! Please remember, statistics sadly indicate that the highest number of suicides occur among mentally ill individuals who do not continue on their medicine(s).

Mental disorders are in ways similar to cancer. As with cancer, mental illness is a condition that can be mild to severe, and medicines exist that benefit both. Unfortunately, these medicines have a reputation of leaving the sufferer with noticeable and sometimes even devastating physical side effects. The promise of success makes both the cancer sufferer and the mental illness sufferer willing to tolerate the negative aspects of the medicine.

Jonathan and I were taught in classes we attended during his hospital stay at Charter that mental disorders are in ways similar to diabetes. More often than not the disease lasts a lifetime and is incurable. By far, most organic serious mental illnesses that impede functioning can and should be treated with medication. Vitamins and supplements can also help. But just like diabetics need insulin, mentally ill need psychiatric medicine.

"The mortality rate for untreated manic–depressive illness is higher than it is for many types of heart disease and cancer".[13]

Patience is imperative in finding the correct psychiatric medicine or combination. Every doctor Ron and I have gone to has stressed the importance of remembering that once you start a medication

I would like to include a warning for those taking psychiatric drugs: be on as little as possible to improve your illness. Take the cue from your caregiver and the advice of your doctor.

that works, it is not a straight road to recovery. The road of healing takes many twists and turns, ups and downs before finally stabilizing. The doctors emphasize to understand this and work with it!

Faith is on autopilot.

Of course, medicine along with counseling from someone who understands mental illness is the best duo for success. Once medicine is found that works, counseling is beneficial to:

- help someone deal with repercussions of past episodes.

- help encourage the taking of medications necessary to prevent further episodes.

- help someone deal with setbacks that occur when living with mental illness.

Biblical counseling is important to help one remember the truths of Scripture and that God is good even through illness.

Let me say that not everyone who has depression symptoms needs to rush to the psychiatrist or go on an antidepressant. Often the symptoms

---

[13] *Touched with Fire* by Kay Redfield Jamison, Ph.D,, Simon and Schuster New York, 1994, p. 41

subside after the trauma that triggered it does. I would first see if counseling, Scripture reading, meditation, and prayer, can help alleviate the symptoms. Becoming connected and interacting with others is also beneficial to relieving depression symptoms, as well as getting adequate sleep and exercise. If your dark hole of depression persists, however, something may be going on that needs medical intervention. Don't delay too long.

At our next visit with Jon's psychiatrist, he suggests trying the antidepressant *Zoloft* instead of *Effexor* along with his *Geodon*. Another medication trial on our son. He also tells Ron and me that there is no hope for Jonathan to get better. This is the way he's going to be the rest of his life.

You know, with your children, how you have dreams for their lives? We have hoped Jon might take over Majesty Music one day. I come to the point where I don't care what Jonathan does vocationally. My list of ambitions has dwindled down to one thing—wanting him to be able to function, at least somewhat normally without mental torment.

Can It Get Any Worse?

June 21, 2001

Morning Minutes

People tell me during Jonathan's illness that God will use it for good in our ministry. Although I am glad for this, I really don't want it to be at Jonathan's expense. I want Jonathan to be strengthened. I want whatever happens to be good for him too. No parent likes to see their child suffer. I share this thought with a preacher friend of ours, Les Ollila.

I will never forget what he tells me, "Shelly, you know God loves your child as much as He loves you. God is working in his life too, to bring him to Himself." These are exactly the words I have been searching for in my soul. Thank you, Les.

God is working something special here for Jonathan.

Okay, dear Jesus, I am going to "put all of my eggs in that basket"—thoughts taken from Ephesians 1:18.

Ron and I decide it is time to try a new doctor. We are hopeful for another perspective to confirm or change the current diagnosis and/or make necessary improvements to the course of treatment.

We hear great things about Dr. Jeffrey Craddock. Dr. Craddock is a dedicated Christian and gives us exactly what we need at the time—HOPE! Over the next twelve years, he becomes our dedicated friend and advocate.

Dr. Craddock gives Jonathan a series of different tests—written psychiatric tests and blood tests. He also refers us to a neurologist so Jonathan can get a brain scan. When we visit the neurologist for the first time, he looks directly at our Jonathan and says, "We are going to get you help."

He prays with us and immediately sends Jon for an MRI. The MRI shows shady areas in Jonathan's brain which look like what you might see in schizophrenics. Despite this, the neurologist has given Jonathan and us another optimistic boost with a dose of hope. Can you believe nineteen years later I remember this brief "encounter of light" in a very dark tunnel?

Back at Dr. Craddock's, he begins a long search for the right cocktail of medicines (as it is called) to help our Jonathan. As I have said, it takes a while for psychiatric medicines to work, some as long as six weeks. There are hundreds of them with which to experiment. For serious mental illness cases, it can take an average of five to eight years to find the right medicine or right combination of medicines (if you can be patient that long).

We are grateful for Dr. Craddock's persistence in helping our beloved Jonathan. I cannot imagine the life of a psychiatrist. These dedicated people choose to take on the treacherous journey that someone with a mental disorder experiences. They accept the oftentimes horror and darkness that comes with the territory, unlike the families affected that have no choice in the matter.

After Jonathan has an appointment with Dr. Craddock, Ron enters a restaurant where Dr. Craddock is eating. Ron walks right by his table and doesn't say anything. Honestly, Ron doesn't see him, but Dr. Craddock tells us later that he wasn't surprised. Most people don't acknowledge they know him in public. This is sad, is it not?

A combination of medications is found enabling Jonathan to become well enough to work a little outside of the home. Different church friends are so kind and invite Jonathan to help them at their personally owned businesses. Wayne Ingram comes and picks Jonathan up to help him do miscellaneous jobs. Some days Wayne barbecues pork on his smoker to bring back to our family for dinner. It is delicious and a shot of joy.

Other days Jonathan goes to Andy Peterson's to help him in his carpentry business. Andy teaches Jon how to carve. Andy's niece loves SpongeBob™, so he asks Jon to carve one for her out of wood. SpongeBob™ turns out very nicely. Jonathan is fairly talented in a number of areas. Thank you, Andy.

Jonathan gets well enough to drive his car again. This is a small but welcome improvement. Jon is able to start working by driving himself a couple of days a week to Chick-Fil-A™ on Wade Hampton Boulevard. It may seem insignificant to mention that Jonathan can now work part time. After the heart-wrenching weeks in the hospital and the unthinkably bleak reality that he may never improve, we cling to any sign, however small, that he will live a normal life.

Like · Comment · Share

Jonathan Campbell Hamilton
November 19

It's starting to get crazy at chick-fila. The mall get's swamped at christmas. Not looking forward to black friday. Luckily I don't have to work the 3 a.m. shift

Jonathan was a dedicated Chick-fil-A worker and loved it.

July 2001

Morning Minutes

I am now very familiar with feeling weak much of the time—physically, emotionally, and spiritually. I am constantly having to lean on my Lord, which I know is a good thing. There are days I can't get off the couch. I am reminded of how Jesus is the vine and I am the branch. A branch depends completely upon the vine for its nourishment, strength, and health.

Jesus is our source of nourishment, strength, and health. Everything we need is in Him—thoughts taken from Psalms 126:5.

Dr. Craddock changes Jonathan's diagnosis to mood disorder with psychotic features. Jonathan's bizarre behavior is continuing to crescendo. Will it never end?

September 14, 2001

My next journaling is in September:

> *Dr. Craddock records a no-show for Jon's appointment.*
>
> *For two weeks we have been continuing to faithfully journal his progress. One day during this process, Megs lifts his piggy bank while dusting his room and all the pills the doctor at the state hospital has prescribed fall out. We have daily been carefully evaluating ten different areas of his progress, and he hasn't even been taking the medicine. Frustration is an understatement.*

September 15, 2001

Dr. Craddock, out of the generosity of his heart, gives Jon another appointment the next day. The doctor's notes indicate the impression is "prodromal schizophrer," which basically means there are signs of schizophrenia. Dr. Craddock recommends voluntary commitment back to the hospital. This scares Jonathan enough that he agrees to restart his medicine. Hospital averted.

Jonathan becomes obsessed with trying to find food to make him feel better. Although the food items change up with time, this fixation remains constant through the rest of his illness. He has a bizarre thought that his body is not digesting food. Because of this, he reasons that he is not going to live very long.

Jon begins a long line of food obsessions. The first one I can remember is lettuce leaves. He stands at the kitchen sink for hours on end and picks apart the leaves, washing and eating them one by one. For the next period of time he eats only butter, one to two sticks a day. He then goes on a search for the finest flour with which to make what we call "bread cakes," a mixture of flour and water that he shapes into balls and bakes. He comes up with White Lily™ flour as the best, and I must agree it is a good choice. I still buy this flour today.

November 2001

Morning Minutes

Sarah tells me a parable about the cross.

The parable tells of a Christian who keeps complaining about the heaviness of the cross he has to carry. He implores God to lighten his cross; it's too heavy. God responds by sawing off some of the cross. The Christian still thinks his cross is more burdensome than he can handle. More is cut off. Still dragging under his load, the Christian beseeches God one last time. God acquiesces and takes off even more.

Eventually on his journey, the Christian comes to a long, deep chasm. The other Christians lay down their crosses from one side to the other and successfully cross over. The Christian whose cross is

significantly shortened, finds his cannot reach, making it impossible for him to continue his Christian journey successfully.

Our family's cross of Jonathan's illness is indeed very heavy to bear. The battle is ever-increasing for Jon wanting to stop taking his meds. When he feels better, in order to rid himself of the side effects, he takes himself off. As I have before mentioned, this is a very typical scenario for a person living with mental illness. Their illness is improved on the medicine, they think they are now well enough to go off, memory is short-lived, and they discontinue them, not remembering a year ago they did so and crashed.

At first, when Jon stops his meds he appears to be better and more like the person we knew before. We get excited for a very brief week or two. The respite unfortunately does not last long. We soon become very aware that something is terribly wrong.

You see, it takes about a month for the medicine to completely get out of the body's system. So, for several weeks the person seems better because the side effects abate, yet there is enough medicine remnant in the body to keep it well. But there is an ultimate crash after about four weeks off the medicine. Unfortunately, I know this screenplay very well.

A big indication for Ron and me that Jonathan is off his meds is the onset of nightly rituals which comprise him coming into our bedroom to discuss his delusions for an hour or two. In actuality, Jon's giving voice to his turmoil helps keep him in reality, but is an indication to us that he may not be taking his meds. We are many times correct. Although we love our son with all our hearts, this continual occurrence is exhausting.

Dealing with any illness of a family member who lives with you can be a true test of servanthood. Being a servant is giving to someone with no thought of receiving anything in return. In my experience, serving a child who suffers with illness is something a mother gladly does. Many, many times I have wished and prayed to God that it would be me suffering instead of my child.

It Does Get Worse

January 18, 2002

Jonathan is now twenty-three years old, four years into his illness. (See page 114 for birthday notes from his siblings.)

Morning Minutes

Lord, I cannot do this by myself. Your spirit has to draw me up; I cannot do it by myself; I have to covet it; My strength is in Thee— thoughts taken from Psalm 84:7.

Sarah tells me: As our spirit gets stronger, the crevice becomes smaller and smaller between the spirit and the physical.

I will be with thee: I will not fail thee, nor forsake thee. Be strong and of a good courage.

—Joshua 1:5–6

Jon,
I am so glad you are my big brother. I couldn't have asked for a better one, and I am so proud of you! Happy Birthday!
Love,
Alyssa ♡

Love you lots! ♡
Megan

HAPPY

BIRTHDAY

Jon,
I can't believe that you are 23 today! It seems like just yesterday we were in elementary school + you were always picking on me ☺ Well, I guess you still do! Anyways, I want you to know how much I love you!! I miss seeing you during the week, but I'm glad you get to work at the Wilds. I hope you have a wonderful 23rd B-day!
Love,
Tara

Dear Jon
I love you so much. I would die for you
Love,
Jason

Jonathan reads somewhere about a man with mental illness who has attempted to take his life by shooting himself but doesn't die. Now this poor man is paralyzed plus endures depression. This script becomes Jonathan's worst nightmare. He tells Ron and me that if he attempts suicide, he has to make sure beforehand he is going to succeed. Unbeknownst to us, he pawns his trombone and buys a gun.

With his newly purchased weapon, Jonathan goes for a drive one mid-January Saturday afternoon. Late evening comes and Jonathan is still not home. We have no idea where he is. When he finally returns, he tells us he has driven up to his favorite place, the Wilds, to shoot himself. He gets out of his car in the woods before arriving at the camp, shoots his gun into a tree, and apparently doesn't think there is enough damage to the tree to complete the job on himself. So, he turns around and drives home.

You can imagine our devastation when Jon finally arrives back and tells us about his attempt. He tells us very placidly, as if he just returned from getting a hamburger. He says he isn't able to take his life, because he isn't brave enough. I tell him the exact opposite is true; it means he is brave. He is brave enough to continue living with his illness.

It is now very late Saturday evening. Tomorrow is Sunday, and we have our music duties beginning with an 8:10 a.m. mic check. Our other children take turns staying at home with Jon on Sundays so Ron and I can continue our church ministry. I remember sitting on the front row of church that particular Sunday in a daze. Ron and I don't want to tell anyone what we have been through the previous night. God somehow bolsters us up.

On Monday Ron and I call Dr. Craddock. We all agree it is necessary for Jonathan to get concentrated 24/7 help from a hospital. We cannot convince Jonathan into going voluntarily. Our only other option is to have him committed.

Getting a child or a loved one committed feels like you are utterly betraying them. Even though you know it's for their good, it is agonizing.

The process takes two to three days. You have to sign and acquire signatures on all the necessary documents—including an affidavit for involuntary commitment from the doctor. The affidavit is delivered to a judge at probate court before finally delivering the court order to the police station. You have to prove that the individual is a danger to one's self or others or that their judgment is greatly impaired. When all paperwork is completed, the police come unbeknownst to your family member, handcuff them, and drive them off in the backseat of their police car. The handcuffing is for their safety. I completely understand.

You stand in your home, looking out the window, as your child is taken from you like a criminal and by your hand. The stabs of grief and guilt you feel are intense. Tears follow.

On this occasion, Jonathan is taken to the state mental hospital in Anderson, South Carolina—Patrick B. Harris. He is evaluated and admitted. Ron and I are told to leave him alone for a few days to allow him to get over his anger towards us for committing him. Then, and only then, is it safe to go visit. By this time the medications they give him are beginning to work, so hopefully he will be in a better state of mind to see us.

Ron and I will never forget our first encounter in entering Jonathan's lockdown unit. We are met at the door by a young man wearing a football helmet who greets us and tells us he is Jesus. How do you respond to that? (This young man must beat his head against a wall like Jonathan.)

I remember Jon's doctor at Patrick B., although I cannot recall his name. He had a limp due to being attacked by one of his patients. In my opinion, I want to reiterate that psychiatrists are to be admired and respected for their dedication to help the mentally ill.

Jonathan stays at Patrick B. Harris for four weeks. We go visit him often and work on puzzles in the community room. Jon enjoys playing hymns for everyone at the piano that co-abides with the dozens of books, tables, chairs, television, and patients. When Jon is finally allowed to come home, he is not exactly the Jonathan we have known in the past but an intensely sobered version. We love his presence and are so glad to have him back with us in a more "normal" state of mind.

I want to say a word of compassion to families who have to hospitalize a dearly loved family member for any length of time. The pain is excruciating. Although you know the separation between you and them is for their safety and ultimate good, you miss them terribly. I understand. I get it.

February 2002

Jonathan stays on his meds and is well enough to go live at the Wilds as part of the cleanup crew. This is where Jonathan receives a golden gift of friendship—George Clements. Jon and George have so much fun together. Their friendship is built on mutual respect. George becomes closer than a brother. Our family includes George as part of our close-knit relationships. I love George like a son.

Left: Nameless friend, Nathan Davis, Mike Thomas, and Jon while working at the Wilds—summer 1998

Bottom: Rafting at the Wilds—Jon, second to last: George, third to last

Jonathan thoroughly enjoys his time at the Wilds. By May, however, Jonathan has stopped his meds again and has to come back home for the summer. Dr. Craddock is able to convince Jon to restart them. The summer remains uneventful, fortunately.

August 2002

Morning Minutes

Sarah tells me another parable about the cross:

A Christian dreams about his arrival in heaven. When he sees Jesus, the Christian asks Him, "Lord, why did You give me such a difficult cross to bear on earth? The cross was too rugged; it cut into my hands and made my fingers bleed. The cross was too heavy; my back ached, and I was forever fearful that I would be crushed beneath its load. Why did You allow that cross for me?"

Jesus says to the Christian, "My child, your cross was specifically designed for you. Your cross was the exact amount of roughness to sand off the impurities in your life. Your cross was the exact amount of weight to build your muscles to have the strength you needed to complete your journey. Your cross inflicted the exact amount of tears you needed to cleanse your soul."

Jesus had the Christian turn his cross over, and what was engraved on the back? Etched in the wood was the Christian's name. His cross had lovingly and perfectly been designed solely for him.

As fall approaches, Jonathan goes off his meds again. We return to see Dr. Craddock, who makes these notes at the appointment: noncompliant with meds; try shots.

We are eventually able to talk Jon into going back on his meds without the shots, and his mood improves. He starts working part time at Majesty

Music in shipping. Although his outward mood appears better, his personal care is still a problem. He stops showering, and death is a constant topic of conversation.

September 2002

By September the meds are taking full effect. Jonathan is remaining faithful to them and is much improved.

Jon is well enough to go back and work at the Wilds as part of the nine-month staff. He becomes one of George's roommates. He loves it there, absolutely loves it. He gets to be in the great outdoors—hiking to the falls, taking rides on blow-up tubes down the creek, and working with fellow ministry-minded young men his age. A couple other of these such young men are Andy Zale and Paul Weaver, missionary to Kenya. Yes, these are great months for Jon.

An individual with untreated mental illness loses most of their friends. For a time after the illness sets in, friends try to reach out. After getting no response, one by one the friends fall away.

I want to express the invaluable gift of a spirit-filled friend.

Jonathan was very fortunate to receive some faithful friends during his lifetime. Evangelist Ben Everson, who travels with his family full-time, remains a friend to our Jonathan. He would come by our home and visit Jon when he was in Greenville. The two of them would go out to eat or just sit in our music room and talk. Sometimes they would take turns at our piano playing music that they each had written.

As already mentioned, God gave our Jonathan another one-in-a-million friend named George Clements. George and Jonathan have a mutual friend, Matthew Collins. The three of them enjoy going to the mall to walk around or going out to eat.

George is a true, godly gem. Jonathan and George's bond of friendship is mutual. George invites Jonathan to all his family birthday parties. Jon truly wants to go but at the last minute backs out. George doesn't get mad; he understands. George is kind, unselfish, unassuming, and faithful—never expecting anything in return. He continues to call, even though Jon is not always up to answering. For a person with mental illness, a friend like George cannot be bought.

And there is a friend that sticketh closer than a brother. (Proverbs 18:24)

When I think of George, I am reminded of the friendship I've read about between John Newton (author of "Amazing Grace") and William Cowper (author of "There Is a Fountain"). For twenty-seven years, Cowper endured the darkness, hallucinations, and delusions of depression and schizophrenia. Januarys became nightmares for Cowper. On the eve of January 1, 1773, Cowper had a dream that God told him, "Actum est de te perilisti," which translated is "It is all over with thee, thou hast perished." The next day, January 2, Cowper attempted suicide by drowning. He was unsuccessful and ended up in an insane asylum.

When Cowper came out of the asylum, Newton and wife Mary took Cowper into their own home for fourteen months. Newton spent days at Cowper's bedside encouraging him in the Lord, taking him on walks in an effort to lighten his spirits. He took to heart Paul's words, "Now we exhort you, brethren, warn them that are unruly, comfort the feeble-minded, support the weak, be patient toward all men" (1 Thessalonians 5:14). Newton's faithful kindnesses were unsuccessful in releasing Cowper's chains of depression but perhaps lessened their hold.

I believe it incredible that in 1770, John Newton had the insight to realize that Cowper's depression/schizophrenia was physically based, not spiritually. "John Newton always judiciously regarded his friend's depression and despondency as a physical effect, for the removal of which he prayed, but never reasoned or argued with him concerning it."[14] Newton once wrote in a letter, "We cannot think ourselves worse than we really are, yet some things which abate the comfort and alacrity of our Christian profession are rather impediments than properly

---

[14]https://www.desiringgod.org/messages/john-newton-the-tough-roots-of-his-habitual-tenderness

sinful." Newton claimed that the impediments of "disordered, irregular, or low spirits" are often "faults of the constitution."[15] Newton also wrote, "a slight alteration in the nervous system may make us a burden and a terror to ourselves and our friends."[16]

In May of 1800, when William Cowper died, Newton spoke at his funeral. He used as the text Exodus 3:2–3, "The angel of the LORD appeared unto him in a flame of fire out of the midst of a bush: and he looked, and, behold, the bush burned with fire, and the bush was not consumed. And Moses said, I will now turn aside, and see this great sight, why the bush is not burnt." Newton said that for twenty-seven years, his friend Cowper lived in the flames of the fire, yet he was not consumed. "And the LORD said, I have surely seen the affliction of my people . . . and have heard their cry . . . for I know their sorrows; and I am come down to deliver them out . . . and to bring them up out of that land unto a good land" (vv. 7–8).

Newton actually wrote a song to Cowper in which he said, "The Lord has numbered the days in which I am appointed to wait upon him in this dark valley, and He has given us such a love to him both as a believer and as a friend, that I am not weary."[17]

Friends like George Clements and John Newton cannot be bought.

December 1, 2002

Jonathan comes home for Christmas break.

December 31, 2002

I journal:

> *Tonight we went to Bill and Bobbie Apelian's to eat. Jon went with us. We came home, lit our candles and wrote down our New Year's resolutions. Jon told us he was thankful for home and work.*

---

[15]John Newton, *Letters of John Newton*, (Banner of Truth, 2007), 71.
[16]*Letters of John Newton*, 356.
[17]"Newton's Song to Cowper," https://www.desiringgod.org/articles/a-friend-in-the-fire

Said he wanted to work on being more kind. Jonathan remains well enough after Christmas to go back to work at the Wilds.

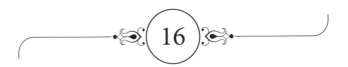

Putting on Long-view Glasses

January 2003

Jon is now five years into his illness. He turns twenty-four on January 18, 2003, while at the Wilds.

After several months, the Wilds sends George to go work at their Colorado location. It is now summer of 2003. Jon begins working on landscape those months with Doug Gorsline. Doug becomes one of Jon's valued friends. At the Wilds of the Rockies, George drives once a week to the highest point he can find to connect with cell service for a "Jon update" from Doug.

July 1, 2003

Morning Minutes

We need to perfect the habit of looking at circumstances through the lens of God's character and not God's character through the lens of circumstances.

We have to put on our long-view glasses. God has the helicopter view; we, only the dashboard view.

Life takes a sudden downturn. Jonathan leaves the Wilds in early July and comes back home. He is not doing well, and we assume he is once again off his medicine.

Jon soon becomes a recluse and lives in our unfinished basement. He feels secure down there for some reason, and it is where he eats his meals. He buys a big screen TV to watch movies and starts believing something alien has been implanted in his brain.

Ron takes all of our personal guns and sharp knives to the office and puts them on lockdown. Jonathan somehow buys another gun, probably a pawn shop purchase. One day, we discover Jon is in Ron's and my bedroom, the door bolted tight with a gun held to his head. I desperately call my mentors Sarah Bennett and Grandma Bell who live across the street to pray.

After a couple of hours of serious trauma, Ron and I eventually talk him into coming out of the locked room with the gun. Jon sticks the gun in his jacket pocket. What do we do now?

I decide to ask Jonathan to go to the grocery store with me to pick up some random thing. He says "yes." I am very aware he still has the gun in his possession. As he gets in the car, I see from my peripheral vision that he places the gun under his seat. Off we go. When we arrive, I ask if he minds going in and getting the item for me as I wait in the car by the curb. He complies. After he gets out of the car, I search under his seat and find the gun.

Help! I need to get rid of this, but how? My time is short. On a whim, I drive to the nearest trash can in the grocery store parking lot, jump out and dump the gun. I drive back to the curb to wait for Jonathan. He returns with the requested food and never questions me about the gun's whereabouts. Another catastrophe averted.

Ron and I call Dr. Craddock and all conclude Jon needs to go back to a hospital. We plead with Jonathan to go voluntarily, but to no avail. The only alternative we have is to get him committed again. We are so devastated that he might repeat trying to take his life and this time be successful; we feel we have no other recourse.

Dr. Craddock does extensive work at Springbrook Mental Hospital in Travelers Rest, so he suggests we send Jonathan there. We now know the drill. We get the proper papers signed. The police come. Ron and I stand in our home looking out the living room window as the police car leaves with our precious Jonathan in the back seat. The pain is again deep and overwhelming.

July 21, 2003

The Springfield Hospital is dedicated mostly for children. It brings such sadness to see them affected by mental illness at such a young age. I painfully remember our first time visiting Jon at this hospital. He informs Ron and me that there is something implanted inside of his head telling him that he needs to kill us, his parents. This is the first time I feel aware that Jonathan may be a physical threat to us.

Dr. Craddock convinces the hospital to keep Jonathan longer than the customary few days, arguing that Jon is a young man with much intellect and potential. After three weeks, the hospital doctors feel Jonathan is more aware of what is real and what is not. He is released on August 14. After Jon's stint at this hospital, because he is back on his meds, he comes out much improved.

October 2003

Morning Minutes

During Jonathan's illness, God is becoming my strong tower, my refuge, my secret place. A strong tower is built for safety. A building structure's resistance to wind, floods, tornados, and earthquakes is greatly determined by the configuration of its construction and by the materials used to build it.

The name of the Lord is a strong tower: the righteous runneth into it, and is safe. (Proverbs 18:10)

There is no stronger tower for the Christian than the name of the Lord.

He that dwelleth in the secret place of the most High shall abide under the shadow of the Almighty. I will say of the LORD, He is my refuge and my fortress: my God; in him will I trust. . . . He shall cover thee with his feathers, and under his wings shalt thou trust: his truth shall be thy shield and buckler. (Psalm 91:1–2,4)

Jonathan goes back to working in the Majesty Music shipping department. Unfortunately, the side effects of one of the meds the hospital prescribes becomes unbearable for him. So, Dr. Craddock tries a change-up with the antipsychotic. Let me mention here that changing a psychiatric medicine, especially an antipsychotic is extremely destabilizing. During this change, Jonathan has an incident at Majesty where he becomes physically agitated with one of our staff, and we have to let Jon go.

Ron and I again hit bottom.

We have a dear friend, LaVerne Joyce Craig, who has played multiple characters on the Patch the Pirate Adventure™ series. One of her most notable is Widow Magnolia in *The Misterslippi River Race*.

Several years ago LaVerne was diagnosed with stage four cancer. She shared with me how the book of Psalms had been such a blessing to her, specifically verses teaching that God is our "strong tower," our "refuge," and our "secret place."

I am so moved by the strength LaVerne has gained, I give the thoughts and Scripture to friend Cheryl Reid and my husband Ron. Cheryl and

Ron compose a beautiful text for one of our son Jonathan's lovely tunes. The resulting song:

The Secret Place
Lyrics: Cheryl Reid, Ron Hamilton;
Music: Jonathan Hamilton © 2007 by Majesty Music, Inc.

I've found a secret place of comfort and release,
A special place of healing, a quiet place of peace.
And everyone who dwells there finds rest beneath God's wings.
In the shade of His pavilion, new strength He always brings.

Refrain

I find hope; I find grace
Far away from the world's embrace.
He gives me rest; He keeps me safe;
I find His strength; I seek His face
In the secret place.

With every trial He brings, my Lord will make a way
To strengthen and protect me, to help me face each day.
He leads me through the valley to draw me closer still.
Knowing even in the shadows, I find His perfect will.

In summation—no one is exempt from the effects sin has brought to our world and deposited on our lives. Sin's repercussions are far-reaching and devastating. Sometimes we as Christians believe we should somehow be exempt, but we are not. Truthfully, Christians are targeted more with Satan's deceitful attacks. What we know is that we are promised that God works all things together for good for His children (paraphrased from Romans 8:28). When I put on my long-view glasses, I can see with more clarity God's promise in Ecclesiastes 3:11, "He hath made everything beautiful in His time . . . from the beginning to the end."

Fake Voices

I'll never forget Jonathan's stay in the Springfield Mental Hospital. His telling us that voices in his head were telling him to kill Ron and me was shocking and disquieting. How and why do some with mental illness hear voices that aren't real?

I started calling on Ron's and my dear friend, Pastor Doug Fisher of Lighthouse Baptist Church in San Diego, California. Doug has been a light to Ron and me during some of our darkest times of dealing with Jon's mental illness. Doug has himself experienced three different episodes of deep depression. By taking copious notes of our phone conversations and listening to a message Doug gave about his experiences, I learned a great deal about fake voices.

Nobody likes fake. We all want honesty, authenticity, genuineness, and transparency. I read somewhere that the most Googled™ word in 2020 was *integrity*. I believe the world is hungry for people with integrity—of good character, ethics, and morals.

What are "fake voices?" We comprehend from Scripture that the anti-Christ will mimic the Lord, putting on a mask of godly characteristics. After the rapture when Christ's church is taken off the earth to be with Him in heaven, the anti-Christ is going to fool many people. He will display a "Fake Voice." Many people will be deluded into thinking that the anti-Christ is Lord.

In Revelation 12:10, Satan is called "the accuser." We are told that presently, day and night, he accuses us to God and God to us. He also accuses you to me and me to you. "Principalities and powers," Satan's helpers—the rulers of darkness in this world—know the Scriptures. The principalities and powers help run Satan's mission to destroy us as Christians. They know the Scriptures just well enough to twist them when oppressing you. Their voices have just enough truth in them to deceive us into believing falsehood.

When you are a Christian, principalities and powers cannot possess you from within, but can oppress you from without. They communicate spirit to spirit. "We wrestle not against flesh and blood . . ." (Ephesians 6:12). They possibly see you at your weakest and whisper in your ear. I, of course, do not know this is accurate, but it is one logical and justifiable reason I can make out of some of Jon's behaviors during his bout with mental illness.

When Jonathan first became ill, I was given some books on demon possession from well-meaning individuals. Sometimes Jonathan's behavior appeared to imitate what I imagined demon possession would look like. In Jonathan's case, Ron and I understood that demon possession was not his problem, but mental illness with attacks of demon oppression.

Satan and his helpers are liars. Their voices do not speak truth. Theirs are fake voices. The fake voices from the darkness are relentless when you are busy serving God or are in depression, mania, or schizophrenia. A Christian need not have one of these illnesses to be tortured by these fake voices. They accuse and condemn. Their voices get louder and louder.

The fake voices put on masks to make themselves give a righteous appearance. Their masking takes all shapes and forms. They can be voices in your head perpetuated by your old nature. They can be the principalities and powers of darkness, sent by the accuser.

The fake voices might even dare pretend they are God's voice. Their voices can warn you *against* everyone, even those whom you love and who love you. The voices from the accuser will bring up everything your parents, husband, wife, or children have done wrong, making you turn against and mistrust those closest to you.

Doug Fisher, our afore mentioned friend, was a reconnaissance officer in the Marine Corps Special Forces, operating deep behind enemy lines to conduct covert direction of air and missile attacks. Doug has had to deal with PTSD as a result. Especially disturbing to him was a command he made to the men under him, putting them in great danger. This command was ordered to him by a superior officer, but Doug still has held himself responsible.

Doug has been a huge encouragement to Ron and me over the years, because he understands the depression my family has faced. He has even had some mental illness in his heritage. I tire of hearing Christian leaders who have never experienced mental illness in their home and believe its cause is always a heart issue rather than a physical one. Doug, in contrast, listens with empathy and wise discernment. Making his counsel to us even better is the fact that he is an extremely kind man. Ron has often told me, tongue-in-cheek, that for some reason he really likes nice people.

Doug went through depression on three different occasions without medicine and eventually came out. Each was triggered by multiple difficult situations and circumstances. All were based on heavy self-condemnation. Doug is one of the few people I have learned about who have come out of their depression without medicine. His is an exception, not the rule. I believe he possibly would have come out earlier and not suffered as much with medicine. He, however, says he was very close at times to taking his own life. Knowing that suicide was wrong overruled in the end.

Unbelievably, as pastor of a large church, Doug preached every Sunday through each of his episodes: nine months, six months, and four months in length. During the weekdays he isolated himself from everyone. Fake voices in his head were self-condemning and persistent. His church and his wife stood by him through each of his ordeals. Weekly staff meetings were set up without him, to keep his church running efficiently.

Two staff members were assigned to be a support to his wife. She could ask or say anything to these two people without fear of being judged or betrayed. Doug's is an overwhelming story of heartache bathed in love and understanding.

Doug says the accusations from the fake voices do not present just speed bumps in your life, but walls. Sometimes the fake voices can overwhelm you, putting you into a deep depression. Or the fake voices can be a result of an already existing clinical depression. They are debilitating. All hope dissipates. You feel like you are falling. You wake up despairing. There is no planning for the day. Total discontentment envelops you like a dark black cloud. During the day you wish for night. During the night you wish for day. As hopelessness deteriorates, you pray to just get through the day, then just half a day, and then just the next hour. You beg God for escape.

Fake voices from Satan and his helpers seem to attack in different scenarios:

They accuse when you are well and busy doing God's work.

They accuse when tragic things happen that are not your fault.

They accuse when you are weak.

They accuse when you are living in the flesh.

They accuse when you are ill and having trouble with healthy thinking.

They accuse as a result of alcohol and/or drugs.

How do Satan's fake voices accuse?

They bring up sins from your past.

They appeal to your old nature.

They give misinformation about something that has happened, accusing you falsely.

Very disturbing is when Satan or his principalities and powers make a believer think theirs is the voice of God.

Pastor Doug gives instruction for how you can tell when voices in your head are fake.

God never announces Himself to you, but instead speaks through His Holy Spirit.

Are the voices negative or positive? Negativity is of Satan.

When you hear the Holy Spirit, you know it is Him because he convicts, and never accuses. "Convict" denotes persuasion; "accuse" denotes putting on trial.

Evaluate the attitude of the voice. The Holy Spirit is referred to as "The Comforter."

Are the voices condemning, either of others or self?

The voice of the Holy Spirit always shows characteristics of love, joy, and peace.

We will discuss how to defeat these fake voices by practicing truth-filled self-talk, conquering fake-voice stuck points, and going into God-directed action. Truth-filled self-talk is helpful, but unfortunately, much of our self-talk is negative. Negative self-talk is so destructive that Pastor Doug begins each morning with this prayer: "Lord, please protect me from myself."

Negative self-talk can sometimes be centered around what others are thinking about us. Doug says he prefers not seeing his audience when he is preaching. He can start focusing on why someone is looking at him with beady eyeballs. Are people smiling, not smiling? He continues, "My mind can go into thinking about what I think you're thinking that you're not thinking, and if I'm not careful, I'll go home and think about what you're not thinking all night long and you don't even know I'm thinking about it."

When you are a child of God, your sins are under the blood. You are not condemned.

> *There is therefore now no condemnation to them which are in Christ Jesus. (Romans 8:1)*

When you are a child of God, because your sins are forgiven, God will not accuse and put you on trial but will lovingly exonerate you because your sins are covered by His blood.

> *In whom we have redemption through his blood, even the forgiveness of sins. (Colossians 1:4)*

When you are a child of God, He speaks to you with His Holy Spirit which is within you. The Holy Spirit will convict (make you aware of a sin that needs to be forgiven) but never condemn (tell you that your sin will send you to hell).

> *It is expedient for you that I [Jesus] go away: for if I go not away, the Comforter will not come unto you; but if I depart, I will send him unto you. And when he is come, he will reprove [convict] the world of sin. (John 16:7–8)*

Lord, help me to differentiate between the fake voices and Your voice of truth!

> *Every one that is of the truth heareth my voice. (John 18:37)*

God's help comes in many forms. Where is your help?

> *From whence cometh my help? My help cometh from the LORD which made heaven and earth. (Psalm 121:1–2)*

God's help sometimes comes in the form of medicine. If your neurotrans-mitters are not functioning, making you delusional, you will be unable to reason your way to truth. If the problem is misfiring of neurotransmitters, please see a qualified doctor called a psychiatrist. You may need medicines to help you first think rationally before the spiritual helps can benefit.

There are scriptural principles you can do mentally and spiritually to free you from fake voices. Doug learned about the practices of self-talk, stuck points, and going into action from the Veteran's Hospital. These are the helps used with PTSD. Doug, as a pastor, recognized the practices are based on scriptural truth and have biblical examples.

1. Practice truth-filled self-talk.

    You have to counter the fake voices. Decipher what the voices are telling you that is contrary to Scripture. Speak truth to yourself. Fight any negative self-talk. As my son-in-law Ben tells me, "Don't listen to yourself, talk to yourself." You might need someone to help guide you through this process.

    Biblical example: In 1 Samuel 26 Saul had been seeking David's life. David two times spares Saul's life when it was in his power to take it. Saul finds this out and repents, telling David, "I will no more do thee harm" (v. 21). In chapter 27, David has a lack of faith and says in his heart, "I shall now perish one day by the hand of Saul" (v. 1). David's self-talk is not truth-filled. He is feeding himself misinformation. In Psalm 42:5–6 David turns his negative self-talk into positive. "Why art thou cast down, O my soul? And why art thou disquieted in me? hope thou in God: for I shall yet praise him for the help of his countenance. O my God, my soul is cast down within me: therefore will I remember thee from the land of Jordan." He goes on in verse 11: "hope thou in God: for I shall yet praise him, who is the health of my countenance, and my God."

2. Conquer fake-voice stuck points.

    When practicing self-talk filled with error, you will come to stuck points—points in your narrative that are the biggest obstacles to overcome. The fake voices make you self-absorbed, condemning either yourself or someone else. If you have repented of a sin, God has forgiven you. If you haven't, it's time. Once you are for-given but still have a stuck point, ask someone help you break it down—like peeling away layers of an onion. If the stuck point is not your fault, you need to recategorize it to help take yourself off the hook and to stop blaming yourself. If it is someone else's fault, take them off the hook as well and stop being bitter. If the stuck point is your fault, take it to God and ask forgiveness.

Biblical example: David keeps imagining that Saul is going to kill him, which becomes his stuck point. He runs away to the land of the Philistines for a year and four months, which is a big mistake, leading David into trouble later. We are told in 1 Samuel 27:4 that the truth was Saul "sought no more again for him." No matter to David, he was stuck on fake information.

3. Go into God-directed action.

   When you start practicing truth-filled self-talk and have conquered the stuck points, you are ready to go into action listening only to the voice of God. Instead of confronting the fake voices and listening to God, you may have felt like David, that if you could just escape all would be okay.

   Biblical example: After Israel is attacked by the Amalekites, David's two wives are taken captive. 1 Samuel 30:6 says that although David was distressed, he trusted and "encouraged himself in the LORD his God." The God-directed action David takes is reinstating his faith in God. Now victory can occur. God allows David and his men to smite the Amalekites, recovering his two wives and the rest of the spoil that had been taken. The fake voices that had tortured David appear to be conquered.

Our self-talk is so important. God says to speak to yourself with truth.

Speaking to yourselves in psalms and hymns and spiritual songs. (Ephesians 5:19)

There are two different positions in which we place ourselves in our self-talk. They sound alike but are very different. The first position is that of feeling unworthy. Being unworthy is a good place to be—unworthy of God's mercy, goodness, and love. The second position is feeling worthless, with no hope. Fake voices try to incriminate you into feeling worthless. There is one small step from passing over feeling unworthy to feeling worthless. Be on guard! Feeling like you are worthless is definitely an accusation from a fake voice.

How do you know if fake voices are due to a neurotransmitter problem? Doug has two answers:

1. You can know you have a neurotransmitter problem if you think the fake voices are real.

2. You can know you have a neurotransmitter problem if you are experiencing other symptoms other than just fake voices. Symptoms of mental illness that accompany fake voices will include two or more of the following: depression, thoughts of suicide, eating disorders, lack of motivation, unexplained muscle aches, anti-social, extremely agitated and/or emotional, pressured speech, no speech, delusions, crying spells for no reason, and so forth.

If you have mental illness, it will be obvious to those around you. Unfortunately, it is not always obvious to the person suffering. They many times think it is everyone else around them that has a problem.

There are people who genetically experience slight depression who monitor it with exercise, vitamin D, and sunshine—because once you start an antidepressant, it is often difficult to discontinue. Some depressions are short-lived due to difficult circumstances or due to a significant drop in progesterone for a mom after her baby is delivered. An antidepressant might be given to bring them out more quickly, and then can be discontinued.

Some depressions, however, are for a lifetime and require continued medication for the sufferer to remain functioning. If you are in a serious depression or experiencing an episode due to mental illness, medicine should be sought as soon as possible.

Negative self-talk can sometimes be centered around what others are thinking about us. Actually, most of our self-talk, both negative and positive, is about ourselves. Ouch! This may be the biggest battle we face.

Speaking lies to ourselves is something we all do—some more than others. And we are not alone. The "big boys," key players in the Bible, dealt with negative self-talk.

We mentioned David from the Bible who talked to himself negatively due to fear. Another great man of God, the prophet Elijah, also had David's same negative-talk problem due to fear. Right after Elijah experienced a great victory on Mount Carmel, he heard that Jezebel was seeking his life (1 Kings 18). For fear, he left his servant behind and went a day's journey into the wilderness to escape (1 Kings 19:1–3). He was now alone with his thoughts. He sat down under a juniper tree, full of fear. Fear is very debilitating. Fear brings fretting and worry and will wear you out.

Elijah's negative self-talk begins. We know it's self-talk because he talks while being all alone under the juniper tree. First, he gave up and became suicidal, saying it was enough and requested God take his life. Secondly, he self-accused and condemned himself, saying he was no better than any of his fathers. Elijah is depressed.

As he lay down in grief, an angel showed up and left him something to eat and drink. Elijah ate and drank and lay back down again. The angel came a second time, told him to eat some more and arise, for there was a great journey ahead of him. Elijah obeyed and got as far as a cave.

Then God appeared on the scene asking, "What doest thou here, Elijah?" (v. 9). The stress of the children of Israel worshipping Baal, forsaking God's covenant, and killing some of God's prophets was too much for him. Now we hear where his negative self-talk has taken him. It's taken him to a stuck point which is a lie, "I, even I only, am left" (1 Kings 19:10).

God was patient with Elijah. He told him to go stand on a mount before the Lord. God sent a great and mighty wind that rent the mountain and broke the rocks in pieces. However, God was not in the wind. God next sent an earthquake, but God was not in the earthquake. God then sent a fire, but God was not in the fire. Does this sound like your life of trials? Can you relate? When hardships begin raining down upon you, they can be relentless and you can't find God in them.

But God. But God then came with a still small voice. God was faithful and there all along. God said, "What doest thou here, Elijah?" (v. 13). Elijah, still in the cave, came out and reiterated his stuck point, "I, even I only, am left." After he calmed him down, God told him very gently that He had a job for him to do. Now we hear God's directed action for Elijah to go anoint the king over Syria and Israel.

God was not done with Elijah yet. Later, in the New Testament, Elijah is one chosen along with Moses to show up talking to Jesus as Christ being transfigured into heaven. Elijah is God's man, even though he goes through a period of depression. God doesn't give up on His children or expect perfection.

Pastor Doug Fisher was not only able to preach at his own church through those depressions, but also traveled to other churches preaching. On one such occasion, he was driving over the Golden Gate Bridge to get to his preaching engagement. He had been in deep depression for months and had thought many times about taking his life and even how he would do it. He never did it, only because he knew it was wrong.

Negative self-talk overshadows truth, making it hard to see the positive.

As Doug passed over the bridge, he pulled over and stopped his car. He thought, "This would be the perfect place to make sure I ended my life." He sat there for a few moments. Heavy conflict was going on in his mind. Maybe it was the negative self-talk that his family would be better off without him. Maybe it was Satan accusing by saying, "You are worthless and not worthy to be a preacher." Whatever it was, he finally broke down in sobs. He turned his negative self-talk into positive self-talk and said, "No! I have a job to do." He had been in the Marines and was led many times by duty.

He started his car up, wiped his tears away, and went on to preach— blood-shot eyes, swollen face, and all. You may think there was no reason on earth he was in any state to preach. He went because of duty and calling, not because of feeling. He said people afterwards told him it was a good message. But God.

> *Casting down imaginations, and every high thing that exalteth itself against the knowledge of God, and bringing into captivity every thought to the obedience of Christ. (2 Corinthians 10:5)*

As negative self-talk is damaging, it makes sense that positive self-talk is extremely beneficial. Some people seem naturally to gravitate towards positive self-talk. What a wonderful character trait. Some are predisposed to negative self-talk but have worked hard at becoming the opposite. I have great respect for these people. God gives us all the ability to choose to talk to ourselves with uplifting thoughts.

> *For if our heart condemn us, God is greater than our heart, and knoweth all things. Beloved, if our heart condemn us not, then have we confidence toward God. (1 John 3:20–21)*

> *Whatsoever things are true, . . . think on these things. (Phlippians 4:8)*

Every time you hold your thoughts up against God's standards of what is *true* and what is *real* and then choose to think on these things, you are loving God with all of your mind. With His help, His Word, and His Spirit, you can triumph over negative emotions, damaging thoughts, and destructive attitudes.

Dear friend, if you have not been in the habit of practicing positive, truth-filled self-talk, do not despair or condemn yourself. Turn your habits! Change your heart! Let God take control of your thoughts!

Best Years

November 2003

Coming out of the hospital in July, Jon is kept on the same antidepressant, but put on a different antipsychotic, *Zyprexa*. The combination is working better for him. The fake voices he has been dealing with are much more quiet. When Jon is off an antipsychotic, the voices speak loudly and with greater power. On the right antipsychotic for Jon, they are more subdued and not as influential.

After having to let Jonathan go in October from Majesty Music, we hear of Shenandoah Boys' Ranch in Calhoun, Tennessee. The ranch takes in troubled boys and is run by Brother James Scott. Although Jonathan is older, Brother James agrees to take him for a time to see if it will help. Ron and I take Jonathan to the ranch after Christmas. Brother James tells us Jon ends up doing a myriad of jobs for the ranch and that the boys enjoy having him.

Brother Scott's wife, Miss Thelma does all the cooking. Jonathan loves her cooking so much that he begs her to send me the ranch recipes. We all get a laugh out of this because Thelma has to cook on a shoestring budget for twenty-five boys at a time.

Jonathan plays hymns on the piano at daily chapel as the boys sing. Jon ends up staying about a year at the ranch. Ron and I are very grateful for the respite we receive from the trauma of watching Jon suffer with the illness. Brother James and Miss Thelma are fantastic Christians who have unselfishly helped many families in their time of need.

January 18, 2004

Jonathan turns twenty-five years old without fanfare while still at the Shenandoah Boys' Ranch. We are now six years in. Minutes are turning into days that are turning into years. All seems one big blur.

Morning Minutes

God may not change your trial, but if you respond in trust, He'll change you.

July 27, 2004

Tara is now twenty-four, Alyssa twenty-two, Megan fifteen, and Jason eleven. Megan and Jason seem too young to have to grow up with so much drama and trauma in their home. Looking back now, I realize during much of Jonathan's sickness, our other children have become second fiddle, so to speak. Jonathan takes most of Ron's and my attention— attention we are happy to give our son.

The guilt, however, is still there because of not wanting to slight the other children. God knows. And I am certain of and claim His promise to work all things together for good in our family.

For a long time into Jonathan's illness, it is painful for me to see his school friends doing well. I really am very happy for them. Watching them, however, as they finish school, find jobs, get married, and have children is like a dagger into my heart. Why cannot our son enjoy any of these normal, everyday common life privileges?

December 2004

We go pick up Jonathan from the ranch before Christmas of 2004. All in all, the ranch is a very good experience for Jonathan. Brother James and Miss Thelma are dear Christian people who mean a lot to Ron and me.

January 18, 2005

Jonathan turns twenty-six years old and is seven years into his illness. Dr. Craddock perseveres and adds one more medicine to Jon's existing meds, *Zoloft* and *Zyprexa*. The new medication is called *Geodon*. The combination of the three medi-

I am reminded that the importance and power of prayer, especially through your child's illness, cannot be given enough credit.

cines are helping Jon be more functional. Praise God! He becomes more like the Jonathan we once knew. The *Zyprexa* and *Geodon* are hard core medications that have unwanted side effects. The results, however, of functioning is worth it to all of us, including Jon.

Morning Minutes

Sarah encourages me: God has given Jonathan everything he needs to accomplish His will.

My prayers are continual, day in and day out. My prayer life has definitely been strengthened through this season of my life. God desires our prayers be not glib or trite, but prayers of faith. Not just any ole faith—but faith that is rooted in a heart of deep trust in God's holiness and goodness.

Ron and I make a visit to Dr. Craddock without Jon. He confides to us that when we first brought Jonathan to him, he doubted that there was any hope for his recovering. Dr. Craddock continues, saying he wishes he could take Ron and me to individual lockdown rooms at a mental hospital to show us young men Jonathan's age who have no hope of ever getting out. He attributes the success of Jonathan's getting better to the prayers of God's people.

I don't find much written in my journals during the first half of the year 2005. David Greene, my brother-in-law who is a builder, and I are able to piece together that these are the months Jon starts going on site with David to help as "gopher guy."

David remembers many days stopping by our house, which at the time is next door, to pick up Jonathan for work. There are days that David has to pour a cup of cold water on him to wake him up. Jon's combination of three medicines causes him to sleep twelve to fifteen hours a night.

Stress of Jonathan's illness is starting to take a toll on me physically. I begin waking up with extreme bloodshot eyes. I wear sunglasses when I go out, so no one can see them. I first try several weeks going without make up to see if I am experiencing an allergic reaction. No improvement.

I finally make an appointment to see our family doctor. He believes I may be suffering from an autoimmune disorder called Sjogren's and sends me to a rheumatologist. Bloodwork confirms that I have this autoimmune disorder. After going on prescription eye drops, my eyes clear up. Although I experience fatigue as well as dry eye, I am glad to still function. I keep regular appointments and try to help monitor the autoimmune problems with diet.

Morning Minutes

Grandma Bell, Sarah Bennett's mother, has for thirty-four years served on the mission field in Haiti and gone through unbelievable difficulties, familial and other. Grandma Bell tells me, "I feel like God said, 'I am going to tie both hands behind your back and see what you can do.'"

She believes God has allowed her to have many hardships so that she understands it is only through Him that she is able to accomplish anything. Feeling otherwise, that she did it all herself, she would have become very proud. She chooses to trust in God's strength and goodness. The results are incredible—the founding of 350 outstations and translating Sunday school lessons and Bible stories into Haitian Creole.

Jon's meds, as well as the depression, have caused Jonathan to go prematurely bald. He has also gained over forty pounds due to the meds. Despite the negative side effects, functionality is better than the alternative.

Jonathan acquires every preaching tape he can of Pastor Mark Minnick, his favorite preacher. He spends hours filling his mind with Pastor Minnick's wisdom from God's Word. Jon also buys *I Love Lucy* and *The Andy Griffith Show* DVDs and watches them by the hour. Many evenings Ron and Jonathan read the *Left Behind* book series about the rapture and tribulation period. They go back and forth, alternating reading paragraphs out loud. This is a special memory for Ron.

August 2005

Morning Minutes

I know God is going to do something good and glorious in Jonathan's life, because that is Who He is and in keeping with His character.

My sister Gina and her husband David open a restaurant just down the road from Majesty Music on Wade Hampton Boulevard. They call it Market Square Deli, and it is very successful. They ask Jonathan to work there, and he loves it. The deli opens in August of 2005 and runs through June of 2008. Surprisingly, Jonathan works every day, 11:00 a.m. to 5:00 p.m., for the three years that the deli is open. While there he even has a girlfriend for a short time. He unfortunately is unable to handle the stress of a relationship, and it is short-lived.

The staff at the deli love Jon, and he loves them. Jon especially enjoys working with Uncle David, Aunt Gina, Aunt Holly, and his cousin Chandler. Here at the deli Jon finds community. David says Jon is one of their hardest workers. He does all his jobs well—A+ work. Jon is responsible for making the chicken salad every day, a customer favorite. He is proud of that chicken salad, toasting the almonds that go into it and then adding sour cream and crushed pineapple.

Depression and delusional thoughts, unfortunately, are a constant companion for Jon even on an antipsychotic. We continue experimenting with different dosages of his meds to try to help.

I meet a homeless woman at church and spend time finding her a place to live, food, and a job. Jonathan tells Ron that he feels he is a burden to us and fears becoming like her, always dependent on others. He again talks about suicide. On January 16, 2006, he actually acquires enough apple seeds to ingest what he thinks will be a lethal amount. Nothing

Hamilton Family Picture, Easter 2006, L to R—Alyssa,
Shelly, Ron, Jason, Megan, Jonathan, Tara, Clayton, Ben Farrell

negative happens. Occasional "taking his life" discussions and attempts unfortunately still occur from time to time.

In hindsight, however, I believe some of Jonathan's best years are when he works at the deli. In July of 2007, he actually applies to go back to college to finish his degree. When the first day of class arrives, however, Jonathan reneges.

May 2008

A song to which our son Jonathan writes the music and our friend Cheryl Reid creates the lyrics is "Higher Ground." Jonathan, due to his depression, chooses the words "higher ground" for the theme and tries to write the lyrics on his own. He cannot make his thoughts come to life, so instead gives his conception to Cheryl.

I believe that Jonathan, by his failure to pull himself out of his depression with his own strength, is wanting to communicate we can get to higher ground by Jesus Christ. I believe through this song, Jon wants us to know that we too can have our spirits lifted to higher ground by trusting in God. Anyone can trust Jesus when things are going well and when they are feeling good. God must be truly worshipped when one of His children trusts in Him when their eyes can't see and the darkness is overwhelming.

When faith is strong, it glorifies God and becomes a form of worship. I draw this thought from Romans 4:20.

Higher Ground
Lyrics: Cheryl Reid; Music: Jonathan Hamilton
© 2008 by Majesty Music, Inc.

Though Satan's weights would pull me down,
The Savior guides my way.
My steps are measured by His Word;
A firm foundation He has laid.

Refrain

I want to stand on higher ground—
To know His voice—the sweetest sound.
No turning back, I'm heaven bound.
Lord, lift me up to higher ground.

New strength I find on higher ground
Above the world's allure.
He marks my path and points my way.
In Christ alone I am secure.

July 2008

Unfortunately, Gina and David's deli closes in 2008. Dr. Craddock puts in Jon's next office visit notes that Jonathan feels he is to blame. My heart sinks. Of course, he in no way has anything to do with its closing. Although the deli is well patronized at lunch, it isn't enough to meet all the expenses. We are all saddened when it no longer exists, particularly Jon.

As is our custom, August is when we record the newest Patch the Pirate adventure. After about six months of Ron and me working arduously on the story and songs, we head up to Indiana to record the orchestrations. The trip to Indy takes eight to nine hours from Greenville.

Halfway there on August 17, 2008, we receive a call from our daughter Alyssa who is at home with Jonathan. Apparently, he has several hours previously taken over one hundred sleeping pills. She finds him sitting in the leather recliner in our den, waiting to die.

Ron and I try not to panic. We are in the mountains, but have got to find a place to turn around and go home. I call Dr. Gaddy on my cell phone. Since it has been a significant length of time since Jon has taken the overdose, and he is still sitting upright in a chair and talking, we are told that he is past the critical stage. There is no danger of him dying. Dr. Gaddy says Alyssa, however, should get him immediately to the emergency room where they can pump his stomach.

There is no question that Jonathan's life is our greatest concern. Our hearts want to be with our Jonathan. It will be about a five-hour drive. So by the time we arrive, he will likely be back home from the hospital. Since Jonathan is not in danger and Alyssa is there to take care of what needs to be done, Ron and I make a tough decision to keep with the plan. Our Jonathan is safe and his prognosis is no longer critical.

Although it sounds horrific and heartless, the suicide attempts are no longer completely unexpected, even though always traumatic. You learn to push through them. We have thirty-one orchestra members contracted to play at Aire Born Studios in Indy the next morning for eight hours of recording. The plan remains the plan. Having to make this decision, however, is a heart-wrenching memory.

Alyssa stays in contact with us and gets Jon immediately to the emergency room. The hospital decides to keep him overnight. They give him a drink of a charcoal substance. The concoction is fortunately bad enough to keep him from ever trying this tactic again.

Aside from the nasty drink, Jonathan actually is enjoying the hospital stay. When we call him, he tells us the nurses are so nice and pretty. He gets waited on hand and foot and can watch as much TV and as many channels as he wants. The inability to connect the dots between what's real and what is superficial is part of Jon's thinking problems. His emotions are also somewhat skewed.

Ron and I realize the timing of his attempted suicide is a month after the closing of the deli for which he blames himself. Our hearts ache! I know how badly I feel when experiencing disappointment or guilt. Magnify this times one thousand for someone dealing with depression and delusions.

To Jonathan, the deli was something for which to get up. His family members working there were his community. Making the chicken salad, a deli favorite, gave him meaning in life. For someone not struggling, these little things may seem insignificant. To someone else, however, whose life has been so full before, these small things are almost everything.

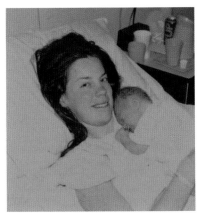
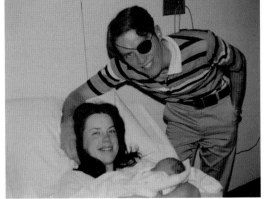

January 18, 1979—Mommy Shelly, Daddy Ron, newborn Jonathan Campbell Hamilton

L to R—Shelly's sister Gina, Shelly's dad Frank Garlock, Shelly with Jonathan, Ron, Shelly's mom Flora Jean Garlock

Baby Jonathan, Shelly, Ron

Proud dad, Ron Hamilton, with baby Jonathan   *Shelly's dad, Shelly, baby Jonathan*

Ron, Jonathan at six months, and Shelly at summer camps—The Wilds, 1979

*L to R—Shelly, Randy (brother), Grandma Alice with Jonathan,
Grandpa Eddie, Dad*

Uncle Dan and Aunt Marty Nelson (Ron's sister) with Jonathan

Jonathan's first birthday celebration

Jonathan "the ham" at two years old

Jonathan playing tennis with his dad

Jonathan with Ron's dad, Melvin Hamilton

Ron and Jonathan having fun at The Wilds lake

Jonathan (4), sister Tara (3), Shelly

Imitating Mommy, learning his scales

Baby Alyssa (2 months), Jon (3), Tara (2)

Alyssa (3), Jonathan (6), Tara (5)

Jonathan (4), Alyssa (1), Tara (3)

Jon with baby sister Megan

Jon and Tara petrified as Chief Hallawaseh ties their daddy to a tree for the "Patch the Pirate® Goes West" cover

Tara, Alyssa, and Jon before Megan and Jason came along

Jonathan, Tara, and Alyssa—feeding ducks at Furman Lake

Patch's crew: Sissy Seagull, Peanut Pirate, Pixie Pirate, Patch the Pirate, and PeeWee Pirate

PeeWee and Patch

Jonathan became PeeWee Pirate on the Patch the Pirate adventure recordings

Majesty Music Catalog cover; L to R, Row 1—Grandma Flora Jean "Nana" with baby Jason, Tara, Alyssa, Megan as conductor; Row 2—Jonathan, Shelly, Grandpa Frank "Pop-Pop", Ron

'PIRATES'
with a purpose

by Alyce Atkinson
Staff Writer

The Hamiltons are a family in a basement.

Shelly and Ron Hamilton and their five children sing at home the way other families eat together. There are two well-used pianos in the Hamiltons' Greenville living room and there's a synthesizer near the kitchen. Dad's guitar case is always handy. With gentle persuasion, Hamilton will break out the guitar and lead the family in choruses of one of his own songs, "My Father's Old Guitar."

"There are many more where that toe-tapping selection came from."

The entire Hamilton family, known to thousands of children and their parents as Patch the Pirate and crew, is accustomed to an audience.

"Patch" is Ron Hamilton, who began producing music for children in 1978 when he lost an eye to cancer. A kid in his church named Hamilton's post-surgery eye patch nicknamed the minister of music Patch the Pirate.

"Are you a pirate?" Hamilton remembers the child asking. "Can I be one?"

That child wasn't the first to make the connection. And the name, Patch the Pirate, stuck. "It was either to laugh about it or cry," Hamilton recalls.

Turning tragedy into blessing, Hamilton decided to write some Christ-

The audiences begged for more.

Soon the Hamiltons of spring were recruited as Patch's "crew." As they grew old enough, Jonathan, now 17, Tara, 16, Alyssa, 14, Megan, 7, and Jason, 3, were launched on this family musical adventure.

To date they have released 22 Patch the Pirate adventures on CD and tape, all with Biblical messages and grounded in Christ-

ian family values. Ward says about a million copies have sold.

Greenville's Ron Hamilton and his family crew have a positive message across th[e]

INSIDE
■ Patch the Pirates can look forward to a new release.
PAGE 4D

The vocals are recorded on Wade Hampton in Greenville, a studio run by Frank and Jean Garlock's ministry, The Majesty Orchestra performs.

Each of the Hamilton children is featured in the adventures by name, and they perform at churches and conferences across the country.

Around the country, Patch the Pirate clubs in church choirs, with 10,000 members, use Majesty Music[.]

Jonathan and cousin Jeff doing tricks on mattresses in our basement

Jonathan is self-taught on the guitar

Eating in Russia, an acquired taste

Paul and Theresa Bixby picking Jonathan up as he arrives from Russia to stay with them in Spain for three months

Jonathan babysitting Mike and Madelaine Dodgen's children in Spain

Jonathan loves to climb the sites in Spain

Surprise welcome home party for Jon returning from Russia and Spain

Jonathan holding his baby brother, Jason, as he arrives at the airport

Jonathan's high school graduation with Grandma Leota Hamilton and Grandma Flora Jean Garlock

L to R—Alyssa, Tara, Shelly, Megan, Jonathan, Ron

Jonathan in the Calvary Baptist Church youth group with beloved Pastor Tom Craig

Jonathan with David, Gina, Jeff, and Reagan Greene

Jonathan loves to go tree climbing with Brian Olsen at The Wilds

Ron and Jon walking on a Holy Land tour

Look out! Here he comes!

Jonathan wins the Turkey Bowl race at Bob Jones University, 1997

Jonathan, Tara, and Ron all ran in the BJU Turkey Bowl race Jon's sophomore year; I of course did not run. LOL! 1998

Jonathan in high school with best friend Jason Hotchkin

Christmas 1995—Jon living at Collier's home with friend Aaron

Jonathan as a counselor at The Wilds Christian Camp, summer after his freshman year at college

Jon and Tara—sweet memory, snow skiing, 1999

Jon and Jas—best buds

Tara with her son Clayton and Jon at the beach

Father and son singing together

Jon with best friend in his adult years, George Clements, at George and Becky's wedding

My five sweet children—all gifts from God

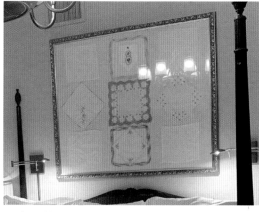

My framed hanky collection from my grandma, Alice Mae Garlock

Jason, Megs, and Jon at the beach—last vacation —January, 2013

Our family enjoys "The Dixie Stampede" in Gatlinburg. L to R—Ron, Shelly, Megan, Tara with husband Ben Farrell and baby Clayton, Jonathan, Jason, Alyssa

Jonathan is close friends with Ben Everson and his family

Pop-Pop, Ron, and Jon—three generations

My sweet sister, Gina, made a quilt for me out of Jon's plaid button-down shirts

Gina painted this plaque for our home

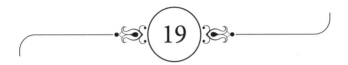

The Beginning of the End

January 18, 2009

We are now into year eleven of Jon's illness. He turns thirty years old.

Morning Minutes

Through the hardship I asked for a detour; but God said, "I am going to give you a guided tour. Stay close to the tour guide and pay attention."

After the deli closes, Jonathan again starts working part time at Chick-Fil-A™, but this time at Greenville's Haywood Mall location. He does well there, although still having some bizarre behavior. He tells us he drives to Chick-Fil-A™ with his eyes closed. O my heart. When he comes back home from work, he sits in his car with the heat blowing full blast, donned with a couple of wool jackets trying to sweat off his depression. Jonathan still remains obsessed with trying to find a food to make him feel better.

Despite Jon's obsessions, the owners of Chick-Fil-A™ tell Ron and me that all the workers love Jonathan. He is funny and kind. They go on to say that he is their best worker. It is amazing to us that all of Jonathan's bosses have told us this very thing. For a son who has spent eleven tumultuous years being so seriously ill, you can imagine how these words of encouragement bless his parents' hearts.

One day I drive to the mall to get a chicken sandwich and see Jonathan. Jon's line is moving a little slower than the others. The man in line in front of me is getting noticeably impatient. I want so badly to tell him, "If you knew what this young man has been through and the strong meds he is on, and if you understood what an achievement it is for him to even be here working, you would be a little more understanding."

Grandma Bell tells me when I lay my head down at night to put Jon on God's altar and don't get him back off. She wants me to think of it as placing him in a safety deposit box and then hiding the key. Under no circumstances am I to get that key back out and unlock the door. Jon will be in the safest place possible—God's hands.

I ask our other children how they are affected by Jonathan's illness. Ron and I have spent what seems to be the largest percentage of our time and energy on Jonathan. They assure me they are fine and do not feel slighted at all. I say, "Praise be to God. Hallelujah!"

I see God working Jon's experiences for good in our entire family's life, making us all more empathetic, nonjudgmental, and loving. Our family's experience is biblical love as it relates to sacrifice, which is as it should be. We are receiving hands-on training. The Scripture 2 Corinthians 4:16–18 takes on new meaning:

> *For which cause we faint not; but though our outward man perish,*
> *yet the inward man is renewed day by day. For our light affliction,*

which is but for a moment, worketh for us a far more exceeding and eternal weight of glory; While we look not at the things which are seen, but at the things which are not seen: for the things which are seen are temporal; but the things which are not seen are eternal.

Trials are appointed to us by God, so that we can understand and enjoy the riches of His grace forever and ever.

For the first years of Jonathan's illness, we had not left him home alone. For these last years, we feel comfortable that Jon is well enough to function at home without us being present. He still lives with us because he cannot function on his own. By far, however, he is having some of the best years since his illness struck.

In John 9 the people asked Jesus, "Because of this illness, who sinned? His parents?" (v. 2). Jesus answered them, "but that the works of God should be made manifest in Him" (v. 3).

January 18, 2010

Year twelve of Jon's illness. He is now thirty-one.

Jonathan's birthday celebration with his family

Morning Minutes

I have learned to pray that God will heal Jonathan in such a way to make him fruitful.

Now no chastening for the present seemeth to be joyous, but grievous: nevertheless afterward it yieldeth the peaceable fruit of righteousness unto them which are exercised thereby. (Hebrews 12:11)

Jonathan during these last years is an ever-present joy to have in our home. He loves to sit at our piano and write beautiful music. Our youngest son, Jason, tells me that Jonathan is his best friend. Jonathan and Jason put on extemporaneous duo-comedy routines at home, which make us all laugh. One comedy act I remember they quote together in a chant:

Jon's the man with a plan.
He's got ten grand,
And he's got a Trans Am. . . .

It goes on from there, getting sillier and sillier.

Jonathan does everyone's laundry and makes supper most nights of the week for us. He makes a fresh loaf of bread for the family almost daily. Jon goes to bed soon after supper because the medications are making him extremely tired. He always warns me not to clean up supper; he will do it in the morning.

Jon loved helping take care of Chloe as a baby

Our grandchildren Clayton and Chloe love Jonathan. Clayton writes a letter for school that says Uncle Jon is his hero. Jon takes time to play ball with him. Chloe calls Jonathan, Jon-Jon. For

Christmas, he gives Chloe a "Boo" doll that he thinks looks like her. The doll has a little round face, dark hair, and bangs just like Chloe. Chloe names the doll Jon-Jon.

Also, in 2010, I start noticing my husband Ron having trouble remembering what I have just told him. I know as we get older, our memory starts getting weaker. Is this all Ron is experiencing? It appears a little extreme.

January 18, 2011

Year thirteen. Jon is thirty-two.

Morning Minutes

Lord, I want your will.

Saying, Father, if thou be willing, remove this cup from me: nevertheless not my will, but thine, be done. (Luke 22:42)

We have come to grips with the fact this cup God has given us is not going away. Jonathan stays on his medicine and has a fairly good 2011.

I receive an invitation to speak at a ladies' conference in North Carolina. I am asked to share Jonathan's story for the first time. I go directly to Jon to see if he minds that I do this. With a smile on his face he replies, "Not as long as you tell them how well I am doing now." I promise to do so. I am overwhelmed by how many ladies remain after the meeting to commiserate over similar situations they are experiencing. They are extremely grateful someone is willing to speak out about the physical aspect of mental illness. I begin to realize how widespread and undiscussed the issue is.

January 18, 2012

Year fourteen. Jon is thirty-three.

Morning Minutes

God stays very close to His children. Being God's child is what is giving me supernatural strength to get through our trial with Jonathan's illness. You have probably heard the saying—"God never gives you more than you can handle." Is this statement really true? Furthermore, is it biblical?

When I hear this pithy proverb, I know what is meant but am always left feeling a bit puzzled. If the psalmist David is strong enough to handle all that God allows to come his way, why does he continually cry out to the Lord for help and strength?

Though I walk in the midst of trouble, thou will revive me: thou shalt stretch forth thine hand against the wrath of mine enemies, and thy right hand shall save me. (Psalm 138:7)

The LORD is my rock, and my fortress, and my deliverer; my God, my strength, in whom I will trust. (Psalm 18:2)

The LORD hear thee in the day of trouble; the name of the God of Jacob defend thee. (Psalm 20:1)

Thinking back over the last fourteen years of Jonathan's illness, I believe God has allowed me to go through more than I can handle many times. The only way I have made it through some difficult situations is with total dependence on God's strength. I believe He puts me in circumstances I cannot handle myself, so I learn to lean on Him more.

Paul says it best:

> *Therefore I take pleasure in infirmities . . . for Christ's sake: for when I am weak, then am I strong. —2 Corinthians 12:10*

Jon and Ron write a beautiful song together:

I Am Weak, but You Are Strong
Lyrics: Ron Hamilton; Music: Jonathan Hamilton
© 2012 by Majesty Music, Inc.

Lord, I come with nothing to offer you.
In my hands no gift I bring.
All I have is my pride and my selfishness
All I want is You as my King.

Refrain

In my weakness now I come, Lord,
Be my strength and be my song.
In my need I seek Your help, Lord.
I am weak, but You are strong.

Give me strength, dear Lord, to obey Your Word
As I take the shield of faith.
I receive your gift of salvation.
I rejoice in the gift of Your grace.

June 2012

Jon continues to do well. He remains sweet, kind, funny, giving, loving, and dedicated to Jesus Christ. People tell me that despite his illness, Jonathan always has a smile for them.

Ron's dementia, in contrast, is getting worse. His day-to-day memory is declining. On Sunday afternoons after choir practice and before the evening service begins, he cannot find his notebook with the choir music or his music service plan. Evening services begin starting later and later as he goes back and forth across the platform and then disappears behind the stage. I am at the piano playing a service prelude, and I look in the direction of the pulpit. Where is Ron? Nobody knows.

November 2012

Jonathan determines he is going to take off the forty-plus pounds he has put on with his meds. Starting in November 2012, Jonathan decides to eat only one meal a day. After six months, Jon reaches his goal. We are all very proud of him.

Also, in November 2012, generics start coming out for *Zyprexa*, Jonathan's mainstay medicine. This means that our insurance company will no longer pay the $1000/month cost of the medicine. Dr. Craddock goes on a search for a generic. None are working for Jonathan.

We research various ways to try to get the name brand instead with no success. I tell Ron we have got to put Jon back on the name brand because generics legally need only be 80% of what the name brand is. Ron responds that there is no way we can afford $1000 a month long-term. We need to be patient to find the right generic.

January 1, 2013

Our family goes on what is to be our last vacation with all our children. We go to Myrtle Beach and stay at Darren Lawson's family condo. While there, Jon gets a bad cold and cannot keep his meds down. I feel terrible that he is unable to fully enjoy the time we have together.

January 18, 2013

Year fifteen; Jon turns thirty-four.

Morning Minutes

Be accepting of God's right to rule and that His rule is right.

Our faith is being tested to the limits. My head knows I can trust God. I tell my head to inform my heart.

February 2013

We continue to search for a generic medicine to replace *Zyprexa*. Jonathan's delusions are getting worse. He actually thinks he can fly and tells us one evening that he has stood on our second story deck deciding whether to try.

Jon starts googling the highest bridges in South Carolina from which he can jump as well as other ways to end his life. I beg him to never take his life. I tell him I will never get over it. He responds, "But Mom, you want me to be happy, don't you?" How do you answer that?

Our family never quite gets off the roller coaster. The ride is smooth and straight for a short while, but without warning, we take a sharp turn to the left, then to the right, a slow climb to the top, and then a sudden rush to the bottom. We know the drill.

I remember once pondering the thought that if Jonathan actually were successful in taking his life, how could I possibly live with the grief of losing my beloved son? Would our ministry be over? How would people respond? Would our family survive?

Ron and Dr. Craddock stay in close contact. We keep a strict eye on Jon's behavior. Ron tells Dr. Craddock to keep looking. Dr. Craddock has contacted our insurance company to tell them that Jon needs the name brand *Zyprexa*, but to no avail. Most people have found a generic substitute, so certainly one will work for our son.

March 2013

Dr. Craddock finally finds one generic that Jonathan says makes him feel better than he ever has. We are ecstatic! When Ron goes to get it refilled the next month, he is stunned to discover it has been discontinued. As it turns out, Eli Lilly, the pharmaceutical company that makes *Zyprexa*, also makes the generic that works for Jon. For some reason they decide not to produce it anymore.

April 2013

Morning Minutes

I am determined to keep trusting. God cares for me and for Jonathan. God is so picturesque when describing how He protects and takes care of His children. God shields us under the shadow of His wings. During the first weeks of the life of a baby bird or chick, it is protected from predators by snuggling under the mother's wings. We are snuggling as close as we can.

Keep me as the apple of the eye, hide me under the shadow of thy wings. (Psalm 17:8)

It's time to go back to the drawing board, and a new generic is prescribed. The side effect of akathisia, along with jumping from one generic to another, is becoming unbearable for Jonathan. Dr. Craddock tells us that akathisia, which feels like restless leg syndrome all over the body, is extremely intolerable.

Jon tells us that one evening he feels so awful that he is up in his bedroom with a knife to his throat. Unbeknownst to us, Jonathan decides to take himself off all three of his medications in an effort to feel better.

May 11, 2013

On Saturday evening, May 11, as Ron and I lay in bed trying to go to sleep, Jonathan comes into our room and talks to us for over an hour. He shares extreme delusional thoughts he is experiencing. You will remember that *Zyprexa* is an antipsychotic that holds delusional, crazy thoughts at bay. Ron and I both think to ourselves that it must be time to increase the dosage of Jonathan's *Zyprexa*. He really is not doing well.

In my anguish, I write this prayer:

Dear Lord, We are looking to You, Father. We have no one else. We need no one else. You are the One. You have made us. You have been patient with our sinfulness and lack of trust. You see that we are dust. You have redeemed us and quickened us. You live in us and give us Your Holy Spirit to comfort us; to give us guidance; to give us hope and a future. May my desires be enlarged and my hopes emboldened. I will trust You. Don't let me do anything to get my fingers in Your business. I want everything I think, do, and say to glorify You. I will sweep all else out of the closet. We are looking to You, Father.

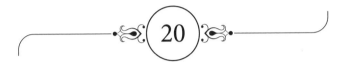

Jonathan's Struggle Is Over

May 12, 2013 (continued from Chapter 1)

6:00 p.m.

After receiving Jon's phone text at church, we finally arrive home following a long, anxious ride. I have spoken with a detective several times during this drive. Ron and I are met at our home by two police cars as well as our daughter, Alyssa. Jonathan is nowhere in sight. Alyssa has given the police a picture of Jonathan. Ron shows them the phone text he has received: "I am going to jump from the garage. I love you."

Now we understand. Jon doesn't mean our car garage; he is referring to a parking garage. He has occasionally mentioned finding the tallest garage in Greenville. There are a number of them in our downtown area.

The police keep asking us questions. I reply, "Don't you understand. Our son is in danger! We need to go find him." They try to calm me down saying they have it under control. They don't seem to get it! Ron and I get in our car and head towards downtown in search of our son.

Alyssa remains at the house in case Jonathan comes home before we get back.

The first parking garage we come to is off of Church Street. We head to the top. Nothing. No one.

We get another call from the detective. He instructs us to go to the police station just a few blocks away. I emphatically reiterate the need to find Jonathan as soon as we can. He tells me they are doing what needs to be done. Please head to the station.

Ron and I reluctantly leave the parking garage in the direction we are told to go. Upon arriving, several very kind policemen meet us there. One of them has grown up on Patch the Pirate adventures. They direct us to some seats in the hallway.

> The chaplain's words replay over and over in my head like a broken record, "Ma'am, your son is walking on streets of gold."

We wait and wait for what seems an eternity. I call our pastor, Dean Taylor, who is on his way to vacation with his family. I promise to keep him informed. Ron and I pray. Certainly, they will find Jonathan soon. He would never actually jump. It is all Ron and I can do to not leave and go search ourselves.

My brother Randy comes to meet us at the police station. Randy and Jon are close.

After two hours of waiting, the detective I have been talking to on the phone and two suited gentlemen enter the station. They lead us down a hallway and up an elevator. It is now that I realize that something is very wrong. My knees buckle under me as we make the long ride up to the second floor. Ron holds me up.

We enter a private room. One of the suited men who is the coroner says, "I don't have good news." That's all I have to hear. My head falls on Ron's chest. Unrestrained sounds come out of the depth of my soul. I wail so loudly the whole building must hear me. Randy joins in. Ron sits quietly with tears running down his cheeks.

It feels like a sharp knife has been jabbed into my gut and then twisted. My heart literally aches and throbs like it has been slammed in a door jamb with no one able to open it for my relief. My limbs go limp and numb. For a moment I feel utterly alone, like God has briefly forsaken me. I feel sick to my stomach but cannot throw up. My chest heaves up and down with choking sobs. I beg for these gentlemen to take me to see my son. They reply there is no way that can be allowed.

The other suited gentleman is the chaplain. He is so very kind and sympathetic. I choke out the words that our Jonathan has mental illness. He replies that he understands. "All our jumpers have mental illness." I tell him we are sure our son is a Christian. He replies, "Ma'am, your son is now walking on streets of gold."

I go to the chaplain, and he puts his arm around me as I cry on his shoulder for a very long time. This man is a saint sent from God. My head is in a fog and my heart in shock, yet the tragedy is ingrained in my mind forever. I will relive every detail over and over for years to come.

My flesh and my heart faileth: but God . . . (Psalm 73:26)

Amidst all the agony, a sweet peace sweeps over my soul like a soft warm blanket. Our Jonathan is now well and in the presence of the God he loved and the Jesus he served. He is free from pain. His anguished mind is now at rest. These thoughts help bring some calm and healing.

After we receive the devastating news, Randy calls Mom and Dad who drive over immediately with our dear friends Ron and Barbara Brooks. As we leave the building, I see my parents coming toward us in the parking lot. I again cry with deep guttural moanings that probably can be heard a mile away.

We have the unthinkable job now of driving home and telling our other children. After we arrive home, we tell Alyssa who has been patiently waiting for us. Ron puts his arms around us as she and I sob together.

We next call Tara and Ben who have just finished ministering in an evening service. They are presently traveling in evangelistic meetings. Megan is also traveling on an evangelistic team with Steve Pettit. She is contacted next. I so wish we had Tara and Megan with us so we could hold them close.

Jason is working part time at Olive Garden™. We decide to wait for him to come home when his shift is over. I remember hearing him pull up in the driveway, me rushing out to greet him at the front door with Ron following close behind as we relay the horrific news. "He's gone. Jonathan's gone." Jason looks at me in shock, trying to fully comprehend what I am telling him.

I have prayed and prayed for Jon's healing. Healing comes in different forms. Jonathan's healing isn't an earthly healing. His healing is more divine, not what I wish for but of the kind for which God has foreknowledge and a preordained will. I am in no way saying suicide is God's will; it is certainly not. I am simply saying Jon's healing was something God knew would happen ahead of time. We need God more than ever before. He is with us—no longer holding our hands but carrying us.

I believe when you have a child with special needs, they become uniquely bound to you by a three-ply cord.

Ply #1 Physical needs that fully occupy your mind and attention because your child cannot function without intervention.

Ply #2 Physical needs that demand hands-on, in-home care and assistance because you become your child's greatest lifeline to functioning.

Ply #3 Physical needs that fetter your child's heart closely to yours in unbreakable love, because you brought them into this world or chose to adopt them. They will forever be a part of your very being.

I am reminded that God did not create sin, sickness, sorrow, and death but has given us a way of salvation. God could have chosen to heal Jonathan of his mental illness as well as prevented me from bearing and giving birth to him. I feel blessed that Ron and I had Jonathan for as long as we did. Jon could have taken his life four other times in previous years. God, when creating Jonathan, knew that he would only be with us on this earth for thirty-four years. I'm just glad I didn't know.

A couple weeks before Jonathan took his life, Pastor Rick Warren's son, who struggled with mental illness, also took his life. Jonathan was very aware of this and talked about it several times with Ron.

You can never in a million years explain in words the depth of pain in your very heart and soul after you lose a child. The term gut-wrenching takes on a new personal meaning.

> *Though I walk in the midst of trouble, thou wilt revive me: thou shalt stretch forth thine hand . . . The LORD will perfect that which concerned me: thy mercy, O LORD, endureth for ever. (Psalm 138:7–8)*

May 13–17, 2013

Dr. Craddock means so much to our family. After hearing our sad news, he writes Ron and me beautiful notes.

> *Dear Shelly,*
>
> *My heart goes out to you especially. Never did I ever know a better mom than you. The depth of a mother's love is truly unfathomable. How you must be hurting right now. I hurt for you. And I pray for the abiding love of Jesus and comfort He can only bring.*
>
> *These are the hardest of days. Days I wish never came. I heard about Jonathan yesterday; I prayed it wasn't him; I have had this sinking feeling in me—immobilizing and overwhelming.*

Shelly and Ron,

God gives reassurances to all of us. We fought hard along with Jonathan. You went above and beyond with your devotion, your calmness, your patience, your persistence, and gentleness. No set of parents has ever outdone what you guys did. Every one of us will blame ourselves for something we could have done differently or better, should have known, should have seen . . . but we couldn't and weren't meant to.

I know Jonathan was beloved, and I know he felt it, too. I know he had tremendous kindness and love in his soul. I could see Jesus in him—an awful lot of Jesus. Gentle, considerate, kind, humble, deferential, generous, faithful, and deeply reverent. I could go on and on. I have put the word out to all of my prayer warriors across the Upstate and beyond, to pray for you and your family. We cried, and we prayed and still are.

Yours in Christ, Jeff

My dad aptly said after reading the letters Dr. Craddock wrote to Ron and me, "I cannot imagine a better tribute to our Jonathan than these words by a compassionate man who understood Jonathan's illness better than most of us ever will."

The week following Jon's death is a blur. Our friends Pastor Robert Graziano and his dear wife Janet walk with us every step of the way. They hold our hands with each decision we have to make. We choose the coffin, choose the flowers to go on the coffin, choose a cemetery plot, choose the cemetery plaque and dictate what it reads, plan the service, create the printed program, gather pictures for a preservice slide presentation, meet friends at our home, and so on. We cannot thank Robert and Janet enough for supporting us through this painful week.

My dear friend Sandy Hankins takes a week off from her personal home design business and stays by my side from early morning till late at night. I will never forget this act of love and kindness. Christiane Emory, another dear friend, stays at our Majesty office to answer the myriads of calls and emails. The Starbucks™, where Jason has been working part time for four years, sends over at least a dozen pizzas. Jason's coworker and friend there, Brandon Nelson, paints a large portrait of Jonathan with favorite Scripture excerpts inlaid into the profile.

After two sleepless nights following Jon's death, I begin taking sleeping pills again so I can be somewhat cognizant at the funeral service. As friends stop by at our house the week after Jonathan's death, I remember talking to a group of my friends gathered in my bedroom. I recount stories of different parents' responses at funerals after the loss of a child.

Until you lose someone very close to you in a tragic way, and even more so when they are still young, you have no idea the wild and furious thoughts that will sweep over you. Some personalities are helped by vocalizing these thoughts. Some personalities keep them inside and personal. It doesn't matter. I have learned not to judge anyone for their first, as well as delayed, responses to a devastating loss of life.

I tell my friends in the small gathering in my bedroom on a day that week, that I have no idea how I will be or act at Jon's funeral. I really don't care. One friend replies, "Shelly, you do care." But I really don't. My agony and anguish are talking.

I cannot predict what my emotions will do. I want to be strong, but what if I cannot? God has given me emotions, and I know He will understand. I know God will be with me. There is no doubt I trust Him with my heart and with my mind. Our emotions, however, can be unreliable. The grief in the very depths of my soul is unpredictable. I can have a meltdown in the blink of an eye.

When someone loses a treasured love one, especially a child, you don't need to say anything. Just be there. Just listen. Just understand.

Family members start arriving from near and far for the funeral. I will never forget seeing Jonathan in the coffin for the first time. I get a chair and sit by his side, hold his hand, kiss his face as the rest of the immediate and extended family look on. The mortuary has done a great job making Jon presentable so we can have an open casket. As I finally get up, my family and I stand in a circle and hold hands. I break out spontaneously and begin singing "It Is Well with My Soul." Everyone joins in.

Let me say that no one is at fault for Jonathan's death. I have relived the nightmare a million times and have asked myself how I could have prevented it. We took him to numerous doctors and counselors. Jon's illness was of a very serious type. We could have lost him at any point during the fourteen and a half years of his illness, but we didn't. I am glad our family had him for as long as we did.

If Jonathan had never taken the antibiotic for acne, would all of this have never happened? I feel a pain of guilt every time I think back on me being the one to take him to the dermatologist. Could I have prevented his illness? Did I cause it? I really don't know.

I have been told multiple times by medical professionals that Jon's illness was so severe and long-lived, his illness probably would have been triggered by something else if not the antibiotic. There will probably always be a part of me that wonders until heaven.

As I have mentioned, sometimes God allows us to understand why we are going through a trial and to see the good that He is working. Ron losing his eye to cancer has had such clear, positive outcomes—souls saved, families strengthened, people called into the ministry. The good is so easy for us to see, the rejoicing so natural and easy.

Sometimes, however, God does not let us see. At times, things happen when you just cannot point to anything good. Pain, sickness, anger, sleepless nights, loneliness, death, and suicide are not good things. God is not the author of these things.

God made us and knows in advance what illnesses we will go through. He paints the big picture, which is artistically and perfectly created. His will is beautifully and precisely crafted for each individual in sight of their awaiting eternity.

Even through life's most profound loss, even when my dreams have crumbled, even when evil seems to have triumphed, I will rejoice in the Lord because He is good. This side of heaven, I will not understand all that our good God is accomplishing. My human mind cannot fully comprehend His purpose and plan in Jonathan's story. This I do know—I will trust Him, because I know He is good.

God's ways are not always our ways. Our job is to trust. God is glorified when we trust Him, not only when things are easy, but especially when things are difficult.

I say with Job:

> The LORD gave, and the LORD hath taken away; blessed be the name of the LORD. (Job 1:21)

Yes, Jonathan had mental illness; Jonathan went off his medications, and Jonathan took his life.

Extremely important to know—those who have mental illness and remain faithful to their medications do well. And yes, it is sometimes challenging to find the right medication(s), but most of the time success is achieved.

Be tenacious. There is hope!

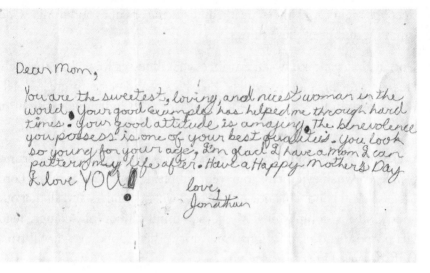

My last Mother's Day note from my beloved Jonathan

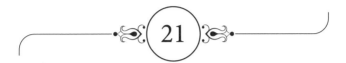

The Funeral

May 18, 2013

Our family has had three monumental events all occurring on May 18. The first was Ron's eye cancer surgery in 1978. The second was Ron's prostate cancer surgery in 2012. And the third, our beloved son Jonathan's funeral in 2013. I personally don't believe this took God by surprise. God is in control of and interested in numbers.

Jonathan was a fine young Christian man whose brief life was divided into two parts: the first of which was a typical active boy who went through spiritual struggles and then became a fine Christian young man; the latter of which was a life cast into upheaval by mental illness, but he retained trust in God. Despite this tumultuous disturbance that descended upon Jonathan at age eighteen, his illness did not define who he was.

During his illness Jonathan regularly struggled with guilt over not being able to exercise the spiritual gifts that were once such features of his life—fervent public witnessing, worshipping God publicly by singing in choirs and solos, ministering at his church, and much more. After the onset of his illness, he was left with few options to live out his faith—acts of love and service to the few people he interacted with and writing music privately to worship God. The few songs that survive from this otherwise dark period of his life are some of my most treasured possessions.

His actions and behaviors often revealed a mind plagued by the desire to act but the inability to do so. His constant wrestling with faith, service to the Lord, and guilt reveals a heart desperately clinging to truth and faith but a mind diminished and weakened. It reminds me of the Scripture that teaches us that our human strength will fail. All we can do is fall into God's grace, love, and mercy. Jonathan's human strength failed on May 12, 2013; but I know that God's strength, love, forgiveness, and promises never can or will.

The time for the funeral finally approaches. My dad writes a beautiful tribute to Jonathan that Pastor Robert Graziano reads.

Reflections on the Life of the Jonathan I Loved
by Dr. Frank Garlock

Some people may remember Jonathan Campbell Hamilton as the man who went to be with his Lord by jumping to his death from the top of a parking garage in Greenville, South Carolina on Mother's Day, the twelfth of May in 2013. But that is not the beloved Jonathan, whose name means "a gift from God," that I knew and loved for thirty-four years. You see, Jonathan was my first grandson, the oldest of my fourteen grandchildren and a very special gift that God gave to me and all the rest of our family. He was even named after my mother and my grandma Campbell, who was a great soul-winner all her life.

Jonathan was born on January 18, 1979 to two people that I love very dearly: Shelly Hamilton, my oldest daughter, and Ron, her significant husband of thirty-eight years, whom I count as one of the most spiritual men I have ever known. Jonathan and I had a distinctive relationship from the time he was born. I would hold him and rock him when he was a beautiful baby. And when he was about two years old, he would come up to the place where I was leading a choir rehearsal at Southside Baptist Church in Greenville. I would pick him up and hold him in my left arm as I led the choir with my right arm. In fact, another little two-year-old boy in our church asked his mother one day why I did not hold him like that. When his mother said it was because I was Jonathan's grandpa, the boy said, "Music schrectors (directors) cannot be grandpas!"

As "PeeWee Pirate" in 1982, Jonathan was instrumental in other children coming to know Christ through his testimony on one of  *the early Patch the Pirate adventures, "Patch the Pirate Goes to Space." Then in 1984, he had a part in challenging other children to dedicate their lives to serving Christ through "Patch the Pirate Goes to the Jungle." Both of these character qualities were true of Jonathan's short life . . .*

Jeremy Frazor (an evangelist who was a college student friend when Jonathan was in high school) sent the following letter to the Hamiltons:

"Praying for and grieving with the Hamilton family tonight. Thinking back on [Jonathan's] life brings a big smile to my face. I remember when God got hold of his life as a teenager.

The zeal and the joy he had. He was on fire for God! Going soul-winning in downtown Greenville, playing soccer for the Mohicans, teaching him gymnastics and watching him flip. What a gifted person. Fun times!!! In the last couple of years, I remember a song that our team did that he wrote called "Higher Ground." It was awesome! I know he is enjoying heaven! He is with Jesus Christ his Lord! I'm jealous in a good way for him and looking forward to seeing him again soon!"

Jonathan's musical abilities were evident early in his life. He always loved music, he had a beautiful singing voice, and he enjoyed playing the piano like his mother [and his grandmother] and the trombone like his father and grandfather. But like many musicians and poets of the past, Jonathan contracted a devastating disease when he was eighteen years old that is very misunderstood and extremely difficult to treat. I am thinking particularly of William Cowper, the great English poet and close friend of John Newton ("Amazing Grace") who [also] wrote:

> God moves in a mysterious way,
> His wonders to perform,
> He plants His footsteps in the sea,
> And rides upon the storm.
>
> Blind unbelief is sure to err,
> And scan His work in vain;
> God is His own interpreter,
> And He will make it plain.

This horrible disease inflicts its victim with pain and darkness that is indescribable to those who have never experienced it. The disease is mental illness, and although Jonathan lived with it for fifteen torturous years, he continued to try to serve his Lord all those years.

Another letter will illustrate the love Jonathan had for his Lord and his desire to be a blessing every chance he had:

"I remember when your Jonathan and Jeremy Frazor, along with some teens, went with my family to visit my brother Jonathan in juvenile prison. Your Jonathan led music and was so full of the love of Jesus. He talked with those guys and treated them with such love and compassion. He was an encouragement to my heart! He was a teenager that stood out to me. He wasn't like many I had been around and seen. I knew he loved the Lord and even through these trials in his life, I still saw Jesus!"

The most singular way that I believe Jonathan will be remembered is for his desire to serve the Lord by writing songs that would glorify his Savior whom he loved with all his heart. He always helped his very busy mother around the house—cleaning, washing, and doing many other tasks that made life easier for Shelly. In fact, on May 12, 2013, the day he died, he prepared a delicious dinner for his mother for Mother's Day and invited our close family to eat what he had prepared (turkey with a special sauce and dressing, tasty green beans, homemade strawberry shortcake, etc.). He sat at the piano and played some songs he had written and one he was working on as we left the house that afternoon. Little did we know that that was the last time we would see our beloved Jonathan alive.

Jonathan will be missed by all who knew and loved him, but especially by his family who knew of all the suffering and pain that he endured, the costly medicines that had a devastating effect on everything he tried to do, and the limitations that kept him from accomplishing what he had hoped to. . . .

I would like to add one more reflection that, to me, demonstrates a major character trait of our Jonathan. He knew how to show love to everyone who knew him, even to the end of his life. Anyone who works with those who have mental illness knows that they often try to accuse those who care for them of not understanding their pain. Not Jonathan! In his last moments, he sent his parents a text message that read, "I love you. Goodbye." Ron and Shelly and the rest of us will always remember and treasure that last "I love you."

Our son-in-law Ben Farrell and Jon's favorite female singer, Sarah Barker, sing Ron's song "My Hope Is Jesus" as a duet, backed by our Calvary choir and orchestra. I play the piano for the service. I feel like I am sleepwalking. We have faithfully carried out our music ministry at church every Sunday for the length of Jon's illness. It almost seems just like another Sunday, sitting on our emotions and carrying out our duties. God has been with us every step of the journey. Ron's beautiful text says it all:

My Hope Is Jesus
Lyrics: Ron Hamilton & Edward Mote;
Music by Ron Hamilton © 2013 by Majesty Music, Inc.

My hope is built on nothing less
Than Jesus' blood and righteousness.
On Christ the solid rock I stand;
All other ground is sinking sand.

Refrain

My hope is Jesus—
The anchor of my soul,
The ruler of this universe,
The One Who's in control.

He saved me,
And He will keep me to the end.
The rock of my salvation—
On Christ I will depend.
My hope is Jesus. My hope is Jesus.

When darkness hides my Savior's face,
I rest on His unchanging grace.
When faith is weak and doubt is strong,
I still lift up salvation's song.

Dr. Craddock comes up to the platform at the funeral and shares some sweet thoughts about Jonathan. Words cannot express the debt of gratitude we owe to Dr. Craddock.

Ron leads the congregation in some hymns and gives a beautiful eulogy. He tells the story about Jonathan and the Easter bunny visit when Jon was two. He then plays Jon as PeeWee Pirate praying the prayer to accept Jesus as his Savior on the *Patch Goes to Space* adventure recording. This is very moving.

Ron and I take our seats with the family on the front row as our son-in-law Ben Farrell shares special memories about Jon and then preaches a beautiful salvation message. The service is over. Our family rises.

As we walk over to the coffin to follow it out, my legs almost melt down from under me. I lean on Ben who is standing beside me. It is a very long walk up the aisle following Jon in the casket to the awaiting hearse.

Pallbearers are George Clements, Philip Emory, Daniel Hendrix, Jason Hotchkin, Nathan Leupp, Dwight Reid, and Matthew Whitcomb. In absentia is Evangelist Ben Everson.

My only disappointment at the funeral is that the funeral home director forgets the CD of Jonathan's pre-program pictures. I had painstakingly put them together to be viewed before the funeral started. I learn, after the fact, that the director drives the twenty-five-minute trip back to the funeral home and returns six minutes before the funeral starts.

Someone in the audio booth decides not to display them because of the lateness in receiving them. If I had known, I would have delayed the funeral the amount of time it would have taken to show them. Such a small thing, but oddly so important to me. I was not bitter, but sad. I realize again, however, that God is in control of even the small things.

Jonathan's funeral is livestreamed on SermonAudio.com. Because of this, we are told thousands of people watch the service. Many tell us that the service is one of the most beautiful funeral services they have observed.

After the funeral, especially meaningful to us are the messages we receive giving testimony of coming to Christ after hearing the gospel given at the funeral service. Other messages are from suffering people who are considering suicide themselves; they are now halted by hearing Jonathan's story. We are grateful for any way that God can use our tragedy for triumph.

It was when I heard about Jonathan and how he died, that snapped me to attention and caused me to ask questions. . . . After

it happened, the day after, I reached out to someone for help my-
self. I had already been thinking much about taking my own life,
but seeing how it affects family afterwards made me fully realize
all the implications. . . . I met him when I used to work there at
Majesty Music. He was always kind and trying to make me smile.
When I share what God has done in my life, I always start my
story with Jonathan. Just two months ago, I accepted Christ as my
Savior. . . . Thankfully, Jessica

Ron was stalwart and strong through the funeral as he led the singing
and gave personal testimony throughout. My friend Christiane told
me that a close relation from California was overwhelmed by the service
and texted her, saying, "Ron is either a fraud or the greatest man of
God I have ever seen." Having worked many years as our assistant,
she confirmed, "Ron absolutely exemplifies the godly character he
has been imparting to children and families through the ministry of
Patch. Though grieving deeply, Ron and Shelly are choosing to *rejoice
in the Lord* in spite of this tragedy."

The Aftermath

May 2013

After Jon's death, I wonder if Ron grieves as much as I do. I ask him, because he doesn't talk much about it or show much emotion. He tells me he copes by going up to Jonathan's bedroom, sitting in Jon's leather chair, and pretending Jonathan is still there.

Several days after the funeral, unbeknownst to me, Ron goes to the parking garage where Jonathan took his life. Ron walks into the garage and goes up to the man sitting in the booth. He tells him who he is and asks if he was there when Jonathan died. The man wasn't but has heard about the incident. As Ron is leaving, the car barrier that goes up and down, suddenly comes down without warning and knocks Ron on the head.

Ron starts bleeding profusely and goes back to the man to see if he has any paper towels. The man immediately thinks Ron has tried to hurt himself and calls the police. Several minutes later three police cars arrive. One policeman recognizes Ron as he tries to convince them he is not in any danger of harming himself. When I find out what Ron has done, my heart is greatly touched. After the fact, we all get a good laugh.

After Jon's death, Jeffrey Greene, Jonathan's dear cousin and I have a heartfelt conversation. (Jeff has allowed me to share his initial reactions to Jon's suicide.) Jeff tells me he cannot help but be angry at Jonathan for the hurt he has caused, especially to me, his mother, by taking his life. Jeffrey has always held to the belief that suicide is the ultimate act of selfishness. I tell him, "Please don't be upset at Jon. I am not. His struggle was so intense for fifteen years. I can never be angry at him. Many suicides are carried out by people who are emotionally disturbed, not selfish. The person acting it out truly believes their loved ones will be better off without them."

Gina, my sweet sister, comes to Greenville for several weeks after the funeral and helps me sort through all of Jon's clothing. The Christmas following Jonathan's homegoing, Gina presents me with a quilt she has made, with much love I might add, out of all Jonathan's plaid collared shirts. It is beautiful. I cuddle with it often, even as I write this book.

Ron and I spend several painful days, about six months after Jon's funeral, going through all of Jon's earthly belongings. We go through every ribbon, every letter, every report card, every picture, and everything personal that we can find. I take all these treasures and put together two *ginormous* scrapbooks. I don't want to forget a single thing about our beloved son.

Jonathan had enjoyed taking walks in our beautiful neighborhood on Piney Mountain. After Jon dies, neighbors tell us they never dreamed of the pain in his heart because of the smile on his face.

We receive over a thousand Facebook messages and over a thousand sympathy cards. Although it takes me months, I read every single one of them. My favorites are the ones that share stories about Jonathan, a very comforting and helpful thing to do for a grieving mother left behind.

Andy Peterson's niece, for whom Jonathan carved SpongeBob, mails it back to me. She believes I will appreciate it even more than she does. I do love it, knowing Jonathan created it, and keep it atop the keyboard on which I write music.

Our friend Pastor Mike Ray sends us a card after our Jonathan dies. The cover illustrates our loving Abba, Father wrapping his arms around a young man. All you see of the young person is his back with God's arms and hands encircling him. They are both pictured in the clouds and the caption reads, "Welcome home."

Through Scripture, we know our Jonathan is in an intermediate heaven— a transitional time between the past life on earth and the future life on the new earth called heaven. We also know to be absent from the body is to be present with the Lord. So our Jonathan is in Jesus' presence. The intermediate heaven is therefore a wonderful place, free from the sorrows of the present earth, but not as great as our eventual eternal home.

The first time I return to the cemetery after the graveside service, I talk out loud as if Jonathan can hear me and say, "I am going to be okay, Jonathan. Really, I am. Why shouldn't I be? What mother wouldn't want her child to be well and happy." And I mean it. I can imagine Jonathan telling me, "Please don't be sad. I'm living in a perfect place, side by side with Jesus."

I am reminded of a mother who buried a young child saying, "My child, I give you eternal joy."

I have believed that God has something uniquely created for those who suffer in this life. I have not the mind of God but am certain that GOD IS GOOD. GOD IS FAIR. GOD IS JUST. I believe John Newton agrees with me as he is quoted saying:

> *[We can be] sure that He is rich enough, and that eternity is long enough to make them [those who have suffered] abundant amends for whatever His infinite wisdom may see meet to call them to, for promoting His glory in the end; for this bush, though so long in the flames, was not consumed, because the Lord was there.*[18]

Shortly after Jonathan's funeral, while I am driving down the highway, I see clouds billowing in the sky in the formation of two castles. I ask whoever is with me in the car (and I cannot remember who) to look up and tell me what they see. Without me saying a word, they say, "Two castles." That is exactly what I see. Call me crazy, but I feel God blesses me with this vision to help me picture where Jon is.

During the last five years of Jonathan's life, as he composed multiple songs, I encouraged him to put his music on paper. I cannot adequately express how grateful I am for these treasures. To date, we have added lyrics to and published eleven of them. These songs are a continual blessing to many. I consider them his legacy—yet another confirmation of God turning a trial into good. Perhaps I know a little of what God was accomplishing through all the pain.

One dispiriting message I receive after Jon dies informs me that he doesn't know if he should listen to Jonathan's music or not. He asks,

---

[18]Mike Leake, "Borrowed Light." Retrieved from http://mikeleake.net/2–15/08/when-the-darkness-doesnt-break.html

"Isn't suicide an unforgivable sin?" After I pick my heart off the floor, I actually feel thankful that this person has asked me his question directly. (I would rather this than see it on a blog about us!)

And so, the question arises—is suicide a sin? I assume that like murder is a sin, so is suicide. As God gives life, He should be the one who takes it away.

> *The LORD gave, and the LORD hath taken away; blessed be the name of the LORD. (Job 1:21)*

Solomon, Jonah, and Elijah, characters from the Bible, all wished to die but however never took their own life. The Bible cites seven examples of suicide. The biblical writers for each incident, nowhere disapprove of the characters' suicides in the narrations. This fact does not prove or disprove that suicide is a sin.

Suicide is not spoken about in Scripture as being the unpardonable sin. This sin, instead, is described as being blasphemy against the Holy Spirit as told about in Matthew 12, Mark 3, and Luke 12.

When a person calls upon the name of the Lord, he is saved, and his eternal destiny sealed. He or she is then forgiven of every sin—past, present, and future—even that final sin of suicide. God has promised that nothing can separate us from His love and that He blots out our transgressions and remembers not our sin. God said, "I, even I, am he that blotteth out thy transgressions for mine own sake, and will not remember thy sins" (Isaiah 42:25).

When God looks upon a believer, He doesn't see our good works and our misdeeds, He sees the imputed righteousness of His perfect Son, Jesus Christ.

> *He that believeth on him is not condemned. (John 3:18)*

> *My sheep hear my voice, and I know them, and they follow me: and I give unto them eternal life; and they shall never perish, neither shall any man pluck them out of my hand. My Father, which gave*

them me, is greater than all; and no man is able to pluck them out of my Father's hand. (John 10:27–29)

I cannot help but believe that when someone with mental illness is psychotic and hearing voices in their head telling them to take their life, God is fully aware of this problem. I will never condone the act of suicide, but I understand Jon's reasoning that his entire family would be better off without him. The same reasoning that he could fly also affected his thoughts about death. I cannot judge but will leave that to God, the ultimate judge.

Amy Richard recently sent the following message:

> *So today is the eighteenth anniversary of my brother's suicide. . . . I was totally unprepared for the phone call I received from my dad's wife on my way to church that Sunday morning regarding my almost thirty-year-old brother.*

> *After Jonathan's death, I sat in a [Majesty Music] workshop where he [Ron] mentioned Jonathan. I vividly remember him saying that he seemed to be living in a kind of fog since his son's passing and wondered aloud if it would ever go away. After the class time was over, I walked up to him and said, "The fog never goes away, but it does lift." He gave me a look. An understanding look. An almost "aha" kind of look.*

> *There is a world to which many people do not travel. But for those of us who have experienced this journey, there is a kinship: a knowing glance of understanding that needs not words.*

We don't often think about the side effects someone experiences after the loss of a loved one—that is, unless you are the one with the loss. I have discovered that the death of a loved one can produce two different types of emotional colors in the lives of those left, maybe even a combination.

Doubting and mistrusting God produces:

red—anger, danger, exasperation

yellow—fear, anxiety, agitation
blue—depression, discouragement, misery
black—darkness, confusion, perplexity

Faith and trusting God produces:

green—growth, abundance, refreshment
pink—peace, understanding, love
orange—excitement, enthusiasm, warmth
white—purity of heart, fresh, clean

A friend of mine, Judy Swaim, recently lost her husband Joe to cancer. Judy told me she has a choice every morning that she wakes up: she can either sing "All by Myself" or "It Is Well with My Soul." She chooses to sing "It Is Well."

We can totally trust our omnipotent God.

- God's will: exactly what I would choose if I knew all the facts—thoughts taken from Psalm 143:10.

- God's way: exactly the opposite of my natural inclinations—thoughts taken from Proverbs 14:12.

- God's work: exactly what Jesus would do if He were in my situation—thoughts taken from Matthew 6:10.

Paul flip-flopped his bookkeeping system.

All my gains become losses and all my losses, gains—thoughts taken from Luke 9:23–24.

> *That I may know him, and the power of his resurrection, and the fellowship of his sufferings. (Philippians 3:10)*

I receive a private message from a dedicated Christian lady who asks me a question that has been troubling her. "Can you tell me why you and Ron prayed and prayed for your son Jonathan's healing, but he ended up taking his life anyway?"

When you receive a question like this, it first takes a minute to collect yourself. But haven't we all been there regarding prayer? My heart is right there with her, and my first response back is: "This is a very good question."

As I awake the following morning after I receive her message, I immediately begin thinking again about the question asked of me. My mind is more alert after the night's rest clears away the cobwebs from the previous evening. I have an aha moment! Why do we sometimes pray and pray and not get an answer immediately or the one we are wanting?

Of course!

It finally dawns on me: what typically happens after we receive an answer to prayer—whether according to our desires or not? We stop fervently praying. In relief, we go about our daily business, no longer as mindful of Him who is our friend and Savior. Even worse, if we don't get the answer for which we are hoping, we unjustly think, "Just as I was afraid of, God didn't hear me. Why did I pray anyway?"

Jesus' death looked bad to the onlookers—His disciples and members of His family. Did God not answer His own Son's prayer?

When we don't receive an answer to prayer immediately and have to wait patiently, day after day, week after week, month after month, year after year, and sometimes decade after decade, what happens? We stay in an attitude of prayer.

> *Pray without ceasing. (1 Thessalonians 5:17)*
> *And be not faithless, but believing. (John 20:27)*
> *Watch and pray. (Matthew 26:41)*

When I mention staying in an attitude of prayer to dear friend of mine, Grace Custer, she says something very simple, but wise. "And whatever answer we get, we must be willing. Willing to obey." How true! This is why Jesus added to His prayer in the garden, "Neverthless not my will, but thine be done" (Luke 22:42). Jesus was willing and so must we be. And what glory God brings about because of Christ's death on the cross—our salvation!

There is not such a thing as unanswered prayer. Sometimes healing is not the kind for which we are looking, but of the heavenly kind. God knows in advance what He is going to do according to His will, according to how we pray, according to what is best for us, and according to His eternal glory and purpose. What He wants is for us is to stay in an attitude of prayer—being willing.

> And [Jesus] said unto them, It is written, My house shall be called the house of prayer. (Matthew 21:13)

We *are* the house. What good does staying in an attitude of prayer do for us, the house?

- We humble ourselves before God. (Humility is always better than pride.)

- We bow our hearts before Him (in a position of worship).

- We are ever mindful of His presence (although He never leaves us).

- We look to Him alone (the One who died so we can live).

- We are very careful to avoid hindering our prayers by regarding sin in our hearts. (Sin caused sickness, sorrow, pain, and death.)

- We search for His guidance daily in Scripture. (It becomes obvious to those around us that we are walking with God because we are seeking His face daily.)

- We stay in an attitude of prayer (submitting to God's will whether it matches ours or not).

I would like to share some special notes written to our family from Jonathan's friends, after his death, that encouraged our hearts.

I remember we were new to Calvary, and Jonathan came up and introduced himself to me. . . . He left a great impression on me as I knew he was only sixteen or seventeen at the time.

—*Terry Foels-Pierce*

His music cheered our dying daughter [Mary Beth]. Your son's life counted.

—*Duane and Barb Wilson*

Jonathan was always so kind and patient with me whenever I ran into him at BJ. He could let me prattle on about nothing with the sweetest expression on his face. Such a blessing to know him.

—*Victoria Hammond*

Jonathan was my best worker [landscape]. He was a very good person. He was everything you would want a son to be.

—*Terri and Louise Kay*

Even as a young man, he always had a smile on his face. His love for others, especially for his family, showed in how he took care of you.

—*Mike and Shawn Manor*

Eighteen years ago today, during our wedding ceremony, Jonathan volunteered to keep the kids so the parents could enjoy the ceremony.

—*David and Maribell Bell*

Jonathan was a joy to be around and had a smile that lit up the room when he walked in. No matter what he was struggling with, he ALWAYS had a kind word for everyone. Praising the Lord he suffers no more.

—*Creed and Kristen Barnett*

My daughter was good friends with Jon in BJ Junior High and BJ Academy. One event stands out in my mind. My daughter played in the same piano recital with Jon. She played the first page several times and finally ended the piece. She was so upset over messing up! Jon knew she messed up and felt so badly for her, he stayed with her throughout the reception! It meant so much to her. Not many guys would have done what Jon did. Ya'll raised such a nice and respectful son!

—Sandy Dye

I met your son many times at the Wilds when he worked there with my son Tim. He was always polite and funny.

—Corina Hager

Jonathan and I were at BJU together. My maiden name was Hamilton, so I actually sat beside Tara in one class and Jonathan in another. On the first day of class with Jonathan, the professor called the roll. When he called our names, he looked up from his list and asked if we were brother and sister. I said, "No, we are not, but my brother's name actually is Jonathan Hamilton!" We all laughed, and then Jonathan looked at me and said, "Well, I can be your brother away from home!" He was always so kind, and I enjoyed that time getting to know him better.

—Becky Hamilton Byerly

Just wanted to say that I remember Jonathan. He was kind and friendly. When I saw him at David and Gina's deli drive-thru, he was kind and friendly. He always remembered my name, which was when I was in college and needed the encouragement of a friendly face. I miss him and his thoughtfulness. I was so sad when he died, especially when I realized he'd been fighting mental illness for so very long.

—Anonymous

My husband and I were missionaries on furlough and attended your church. My daughter didn't have many friends in the youth group, as she didn't go to any of their schools. But your Jonathan and I believe Alyssa were friendly to her and encouraged her to one outing with the youth group. They took her under their wings. . . . She hasn't forgotten their kindness to her.

—Dana Martin

Probably my most meaningful letter I read after Jon's passing is written by our son Jason, Jon's brother

My friend and brother. It will do me good to write. I am writing you here because there is so much I have always wanted to say and never did.

I hope in God's strange ways He might allow you to know these things that I will say here, even from where you are now . . .

When I am asked to describe my childhood friend to people, a phrase comes to mind—compassionately mischievous and coura-geously caring . . .

God has a funny way of doing things. He allows us to each carry our own burden. Some carry heavier burdens than others. Your strength was amazing to carry it so long as you did. Had I carried yours, I would have run out of strength years ago.

I will never fully know your burden or pains, but I will always fully know your love and true heart. Your memory will now for-ever be in my heart, every day from here to my end. I am sorry it was not before. You encompassed my youth and were a source of my joy. Though I drifted from you, you are and will always be my friend and brother.

—Your brother, Jason

To Judge or Not to Judge

April 2020

A stigma has long existed regarding mental illness, although its hold is lightening considerably. Many preconceptions and misconceptions have flooded society. Should you judge the people, doctors, and particulars surrounding mental health issues or not? Read on and you decide.

First of all, there is a preconception regarding psychiatrists. Psychiatrists have an earned MD and specialize in the area of mental illness. They deal medically with mental illness on a daily basis and not with the outdated Sigmund Freud psychoanalysis methods. Psychiatrists have more knowledge and experience in mental illness than other doctors. Ron and I are fortunate to have been directed to a psychiatrist who not only has a deep understanding of mental illness but is also a fellow believer. Our beloved Dr. Jeffrey Craddock is one of the most dedicated Christians we know. He has prayed with us and cried with us. He stops by his church on the way home from his office to kneel in prayer for those who suffer.

Dr. Craddock chooses (and I repeat *chooses*) to give his life to help those afflicted by some form of mental health. He chooses to work in mental hospitals. He also chooses to work with alcoholics trying to recover. Dr. Craddock is worthy of high respect. I have recommended a number of people to him who are struggling with mental health issues. Many have been helped—either with medicine or by being referred to a counselor (biblical and otherwise), a neurologist, or an integrative physician. Foremost he bathes his patients in prayer.

Jeffrey Craddock has become a very dear friend to Ron and me. He presently is housing a seminary student from Africa. This young man wants to get further biblical training so he can go back to Kenya and be a pastor. Recently he told Jeff that his seminary professor doesn't like psychiatrists. He said that his teacher believes psychiatrists are quacks.

I really am grieved that this belief is still possible today and regret the damage I believe this professor is doing. For people like Ron and me who had a son who suffered and was helped by a psychiatrist, this vocalized opinion to multiple seminary students from a professor is sad indeed.

Is the belief that psychiatrists are quacks a misconception? You decide.

Secondly, there is a preconception by close family members and friends. I believe a basic human need is that to be understood. When you are the one misunderstood, your natural instinct is to try to explain yourself. It is very easy to misunderstand and question the motives of those around us, especially those with whom we live. Misunderstanding by close family members becomes particularly sad for a mental illness sufferer.

The bigger-than-life kingpins in the mental disorders arena tend to center around paranoia of perceived failure by the sufferer. The paranoia is real that contact with someone unfamiliar or a crowd of "someones" will end in failure. It is extremely frightening to perceive that those around you think something is mentally wrong with you. *Embarrassing* is the thought. Loved ones must understand this issue that their loved one lives with and adjust their expectations.

Family members of those with mental illness sometimes do not realize that beside the symptoms of the illness itself, medicines that diminish delusions and depression also create foggy thoughts and extreme fatigue. Unclear thinking and exhaustion undoubtedly influence actions and speech. Also, following episodes of mania or depression, the sufferer oftentimes becomes overly focused on doing everything possible to avoid another episode—from fear of personal conversations, fear of crowds, eating obsessions, buying obsessions, and so forth.

Those with a mental disorder can be judged by a family member as being selfish, undisciplined, unspiritual, and lazy. When an individual's mental processes are compromised, it is often difficult for them to focus, to accomplish daily duties, or to make decisions. Be extremely cautious and avoid judging the motives of a loved one with mental illness. It is very difficult for the one who is judged and misunderstood.

I have unfortunately witnessed people with mental illness who are critiqued negatively by a sibling, parent, parent-in-law, or spouse. These onlookers often do not quite understand the illness and may even refuse to. More and more I see why a psychiatric nurse came up and talked to me after I spoke at a conference on Jon's illness. This nurse was most impressed by the love and understanding Ron and I gave Jonathan and by keeping him in our home. She continued that this was absolutely the best thing we could have done. The reason: she had seen many people with mental illness completely abandoned by their family.

I shudder to think of these poor individuals. Not only do they suffer in their minds, but they are unwanted by the very ones who should embrace them. Many who live homeless on our American streets are these people. Prisons in the United States are also filled with these individuals. Something needs to be done. The cost to our country would be much less to house them in mental facilities rather than in jail.

Over the past twenty years, I have heard from caregivers all over the world who have a loved one touched by mental illness. Most are dealing to the best of their ability with the illness of their family member, but they are in need of support, advice, and encouragement.

Some I have heard from have a family member, who on a medicinal trial became worse and then took their life. Some have gone to a well-meaning Christian counselor, who repeatedly counseled them to forgo medical treatment, and then they ended up taking their life. Some regretfully became so ill, it was too late for medicine to help, so they were destined to live the remainder of their life in a mental institution. These are the sad stories.

In contrast, I hear about many success stories, although the journey is most always challenging. I want to give a shout out to the unselfish and patient caregivers I know. I am very much in awe and respect of the gracious way in which they have taken care of their family member(s) who have dealt with and continue to deal with mental illness. Despite the negative aspects when their loved one is ill, they have faithfully and with unbelievable kindness looked to the needs of the one they care for. I have seen this type of agape love firsthand from parents, spouses, and siblings. Blessings on you, my dear Christian brothers and sisters.

Is the belief that a family member is lazy and selfish a misconception? You decide.

Thirdly, there is a misconception by onlookers. Anyone who lives with a serious sickness of any kind is in need of love, care, and respect. Those with a mental disorder are particularly vulnerable. Kindness should always be the signature of Christian-to-Christian living. We know God gives us unconditional love when we are not at our best. We should give no less, especially to those who are ill.

My Uncle Vic, Dad's brother who has a PhD in psychology, perceptively writes, "If you suffer from depression, you understand the added torment of having well-meaning people around you tell you to 'pull yourself together,' 'stop being such a pessimist,' 'count your blessings,' and 'stop feeling sorry for yourself.' This leaves the sufferer utterly alone."

I purposely choose not to judge anyone until I have been in their shoes. (Really, not even then.) It is not an exaggeration to say I have talked with hundreds of people who live with mental illness or are a caregiver of one. Why do they come to me? They know I will understand them, love them, and not judge them or their loved one. Just as I don't want to be misinterpreted, I even more don't want to misinterpret the heart of someone who lives day in and day out with mental fog, confused thoughts, delusions, anxiety, and/or paranoia. I refuse to do so!

Are the mentally ill simply unable to pull themselves together on their own? You decide.

What's Spiritual, What's Not?

The Bible

The Bible is the basis of all that we as Christians believe and for that which we stand. The Bible does not specifically mention mental illness, as it does not mention diabetes, cancer, or Alzheimer's. What we know from Scripture is that all sickness exists due to sin. When an illness presents itself, God chooses sometimes to heal and sometimes not to heal.

> **I firmly believe that even in mental illness, God will be glorified and Christ's power will rest on the sufferer.**

Paul suffered with a "thorn in the flesh" all his life, which some scholars believe was an eye problem. He asked God three times for healing. God's answer was:

> *My grace is sufficient for thee: for my strength is made perfect in weakness. Most gladly therefore will I rather glory in my infirmities, that the power of Christ may rest upon me. (2 Corinthians 12:9)*

Many Bible scholars believe that David's words in the book of Psalms show that he struggled with depression symptoms: the health of his countenance was not good, he was troubled and perplexed on every side, he wept, he didn't eat.

> *My tears have been my meat day and night, while they continually say unto me, Where is thy God? (Psalm 42:3)*

Yet King David is referred to as a man after God's own heart. He trusted in God, crying out:

> *Why art thou cast down, O my soul? And why art thou disquieted in me? hope thou in God: for I shall yet praise him, who is the health of my countenance, and my God. (Psalm 42:11)*

By mentioning David's bouts of depression, I am not giving Christians the excuse to be gloomy and unhappy. Most of us can live the majority of our lives victoriously—in His power, joyful, and in such a way that others will be attracted to the gospel. There are those, unfortunately, who live with illnesses that affect the emotions and the mind.

So how do we interpret 2 Timothy 1:7, "*For God hath not given us the spirit of fear; but of power and of love, and of a sound mind*"?

How? If we believe all sickness is because of Satan, we will understand that mental illness and fear is not from God. God in the above passage, however, felt it worth telling us so.

The Reasoning

At the time of this writing, my husband has dementia. The early signs started about ten years ago when Ron was sixty years old. This is another story for another time. Let me suffice to say that Ron's frontotemporal dementia has completely changed his behavior, language, emotions, and memory. He says things and does things he would never have said or done before. His brain is matter-of-factly compromised by illness.

Can you imagine telling someone affected behaviorally with Alzheimer's disease, Down's syndrome, a brain aneurysm, autism, frontal brain cancer, or dementia that they are at fault for having their illness because they are not spiritual enough? Some brain conditions are primarily deciphered and diagnosed by observing behavior, although most of them have or will develop other physical attributes.

It is ironic that people seem to understand Alzheimer's disease and dementia, both of which deteriorate and take away the mental ability and acuity of its victims. No one would dare blame the sufferer for having it or question its severity. Yet other mental illnesses seem to have outspoken critics and skeptics.

The actions of mentally ill and dementia patients may sometimes appear like spiritual immaturity. Alzheimer's patients can often become angry and aggressive, even when they never exhibited such traits prior to the disease. Dementia patients lose interest and attention to most things, including spiritual pursuits. Persons with mental illness likewise often exhibit erratic and uncharacteristic behavior caused by their ailment. A specialist can usually ascertain the difference.

Believing that my son Jonathan's schizophrenia is a spiritual problem would be comparable to believing that my husband Ron's dementia is also. Both involve thinking and behavior. An MRI reveals some of the illness, but even that doesn't paint a full picture. It almost takes a full autopsy to receive a complete diagnosis.

It is very difficult to decipher all the depths of mental illness or dementia —what is spiritual and what is not. What I know personally is my son's and husband's behaviors and personalities before and after the onset of their particular illnesses. Drastic and inexplicable changes occurred in both scenarios.

One weekend during Jonathan's illness, Ron and I drove down to Atlanta for an overnight getaway. On our trip back home, we heard Dr. James Dobson interviewing a woman on the radio. The woman was the mother of a thirty-year-old son who was living in a long-term mental facility with no hope of release. Psychotropic medicines were not helping his illness at all.

A few years earlier, her son had escaped the facility and while crossing a highway was hit by a car. The resulting head trauma shockingly caused his mental illness to abate. Her son was his normal self, able to get a job, and even got engaged to a lovely girl. After a couple years of respite, unfortunately, his mental illness came back with a vengeance. He was now back in the hospital for an undeterminable amount of time.

The Problem

A person with an illness that affects his mind does and says things that are difficult to decipher between what is spiritual and what is not. Our spiritual, physical, and mental bodies are intertwined. One affects the other. When an underlying mental illness is present, the spiritual and emotional aspects are greatly impaired. I understand the difficulties in separating behavior stemming from the malfunctions of the mind from behaviors stemming from a person's spiritual choices.

I have publicly shared Jonathan's story now at least fifty times—at ladies' retreats, on television and at radio interviews, at Sunday schools, and at conferences of all

> **There is light at the end of your tunnel of darkness!**

kinds. Every time I share his story, I stay and listen to various personal testimonies for a long period afterwards. Caregivers and those with mental illness are desperate for help and understanding. They are so thankful that I am willing to openly talk about the reality of organic mental illness.

Mental health has been so stigmatized and misunderstood and the sufferers so often alienated and marginalized, that the pain runs deep. Those who suffer and their caregivers often feel like they are the only people in the world who are trapped in this valley. A mental health disorder should not be an embarrassment. Many more onlookers are now understanding the physical aspects of the illness. I am part of the kicking-the-stigma bandwagon.

It's okay to not be okay.

After speaking at one conference in Ohio, a lady told me afterwards, through tears, that her oldest daughter who suffered with mental illness lived with her. This lady had never shared the situation with anyone at her church, and so she and her family suffered alone. Fortunately, I knew the pastor of the church had a sister who suffered from depression. Although I did not tell her the details, I was able to share with her that he would definitely be understanding and supportive.

Ron and I know a spiritually minded Christian woman from our former church who had schizophrenia. I one time visited her when she had to be committed in a mental facility. When off her meds, she would go into psychosis. When she was on her meds, however, she was totally functioning and God-fearing. Her husband consulted with us. When she was ill, it was more than he could take. We tried to encourage him to remain faithful, but he unfortunately divorced her and remarried another woman.

Once Jonathan sat under the teaching of a professor that actually ridiculed the medicines given for mental illness. This teacher made his students feel that those who claimed mental illness as the source of their problems were weak. His attitude made it very difficult for us to later convince Jonathan to take his medicine. The teacher mentioned, like a small caveat, that there *might* be a few exceptions.

I have been asked how you can tell if your mental illness is organic or just temporarily ignited by a traumatic trigger. I don't know if it really matters which it is. If your daily functioning is impeded for more than a week or two, I would get myself to a doctor to see if there is something medically occurring which is affecting my brain and behaviors. Next, I would see a recommended psychiatrist to monitor you until you are feeling "back to normal." The risk of suicide and continuing to not function is too high not to.

As with cancer, if you observe something is going physically wrong with your body, I suggest getting to a doctor right away. The sooner you address the problem, the better your long-term prognosis. The same is true with something going wrong with your brain. Get to a doctor! I definitely recommend biblical counseling in both cases to help you get through it. But if the counselor does not believe in cancer, he will not be a help but a harm. Copy that for mental illness.

The Biblical Counselor

I want to be clear. I believe in Christian counseling with my whole heart. I know and love many who spend their life dedicated to help the church with daily living and heart issues. We live our lives in accordance with scriptural commands and principles. Therefore, it is always helpful to get biblical counseling when needed.

I am disappointed, however, with the few counselors who refuse to believe that mental illness exists, thus discouraging psychotropic medicines. The number of counselors not believing in the legitimacy of the physical causes of mental illness may be few, and what constitutes few is questionable. The "few," however, have negatively impacted far too many mental health cases.

In my morning sessions with Sarah Bennett who met with me daily to give biblical counsel, how can I not believe in its power? Sarah is an example of 2 Corinthians 8:4.

> *Praying us with much intreaty that we would receive the gift, and take upon us the fellowship of the ministering to the saints.*

Although Sarah's encouragements from the Bible strengthened my faith, I still remained unable to sleep at night or to stop crying. I eventually, early on during Jon's illness, went on an antidepressant which helped me with these physical issues as Sarah's daily briefings were helping my spiritual issues.

In my experience with Jon, his ancestors, and others, when mental illness is present and someone is manic, delusional, and/or paranoid, counsel of any kind rarely makes a dent. In cases of people with a mental disorder, counseling when not combined with medicine or other physical treatments, much of the time goes nowhere.

Counsel may seem to work for a short while, a precious little while, but very soon afterwards, the mental illness is right back to where it started. Of course, as with anything, there are exceptions. Interesting that in my twenty-two years of hearing from hundreds of testimonies, I have not personally heard of an ongoing clinical mental illness being cured by counsel alone.

In fact, counseling alone, "without medication, is usually considered to be malpractice."[19]

Because some have experienced a form of depression or obsessive/compulsive behavior caused by an emotional experience or spiritual/moral choice, and then received success with counsel alone, they may have a skewed view of organic mental illness. These individuals can still remain clueless as to what clinical depression, bipolar, or schizophrenia can be like for someone destined to live with it. There are depressions and manias that have lifts to normalcy, but more often than not, if the illness is organic, these individuals revert back to the illness's symptoms.

I am aware of cases where Christian counselors have been able to help people with obsessive-compulsive disorder, mild depression, eating disorders, traumatic stress disorders, anxiety disorders, and other issues of the mind. I am very glad and grateful this is the case, and I applaud them for their vital work. But some of these counselors have helped just enough people to become dangerous when trying to help critical mentally ill people. Testimonies by those who observe someone 24/7 with mental illness help validate that medicine is usually the equation for success. I need to add that I have heard of several individuals who had one episode and never had another. I am thankful for their situation.

We can again draw a parallel between cancer and mental illness. There are a lot of well-meaning people who have helped cancer victims try a

---

[19]Kay Redfield Jamison, *Touched with Fire* (New York: Simon & Schuster Inc., 1993), 7.

natural approach as opposed to medicine and chemotherapy to combat their disease. Gratefully, some are helped and even healed. But some of these patients end up dying because they refuse the medical help that is available. I have had several close friends with cancer to whom this has happened. I have learned about some with mental illness who have ended up dying as well because of not receiving medical help.

My husband Ron's hospice chaplain, Jeff, was married to a woman suffering with bipolar. She committed suicide by jumping from a mall parking garage just three years and two children into their marriage. This young couple was attending a seminary that taught mental illness was a result of spiritual dysfunction and sin. Jeff says his wife was counseled by these well-meaning individuals to trust God and go off her medicine. Tragically, she did. This is only one story of many that has been told to me.

You have to forgive me; I have encountered godly people who fail to understand the severity of chronic mental illness as an organic disease. This is in part why I feel the need to advocate for those who live with it.

I cannot, and will not, ignore my husband's advice, who (pre-dementia) admonished me not to judge those who do not see mental illness as we have come to see it. Ron felt that before he personally experienced our son's depression/schizophrenia, he also thought mental illness was spiritually related. Ron reminded me that the naysayers haven't had to live through what we have. I choose not to judge anyone who believes chronic mental illness can be fixed solely with biblical counseling. I don't want to judge them anymore than I want them to judge the mentally ill.

On one occasion, our child was "out of mind" and went to a well-known Christian counselor. No matter what Scripture the counselor gave, the circular ill-reasoning and pressured speech was out of control. This counselor, who should have known better, ascertained that the mental illness was due to spiritual immaturity. I wanted to respond (but of course did not), "Spiritual immaturity is genetic, on their mother's side."

Because Christians still exist that categorize many, if not all, mental disorders as spiritual problems, I am better able to understand why some sufferers refuse to tell anyone of their own personal situation. They are fearful of being judged. This unfortunate fact is the reason so many sufferers and caregivers have encouraged me to write this book.

We tried for the first six or more months of Jon's illness to solely go the Christian counsel route. We had no preconception not to. Although Jon received excellent biblical counsel from these three men, there was no improvement to his illness. And remember, all these men believed Jonathan's depression was spiritually induced.

Jon's brain chemicals were instead out of whack, and he was in desperate need of medical attention. Though counseling can be a great support, it should never be used as a substitute for medical treatment for the chronically mentally ill. The brain, which is an organ, and the mind, consisting of the spirit, will, and emotions, are two different entities. The brain is the physical place where the mind resides. Mental illness is *not* a spiritual problem. You may have mental illness *and* a spiritual problem, but the spiritual problem most likely did not cause your mental illness. If the brain is sick, it will most certainly affect the mind which is the center of the thought processes of reason. The good news is that 80–90% of people that seek medical help are treated successfully with therapy and/or medication.[20]

Biblical counselors, you are so important! Please be aware of your power and responsibility to the mentally ill. Imagine giving medical advice or treatment without training to accurately diagnose a patient. If you ignore the medical aspect of the disease, you could, and likely would, cause much more harm than good.

On another occasion, Ron and I sat in a church service where the speaker was a biblical counselor. He mentioned a lady he had counseled whose son had been diagnosed with schizophrenia. The lady asked him if he thought schizophrenia was genetic because her uncle also had it. A few people behind Ron and me laughed out loud.

---

[20]https://www.psychiatry.org/patients-families/depression/what-is-depression

Ron had to hold my hand to stay seated and not leave the room. I wanted to turn around and say, "If you had a son with schizophrenia whose family line had been touched with mental illness, you would not dare snicker. It is far from a laughing matter." I was disappointed that the speaker did not address this disrespectful response.

I certainly do not want to paint all preachers and Christian counselors with one broad stroke. Many have an understanding of mental illness and recommend medicine when needed in combination with biblical counselling. I merely desire to warn biblical counselors against the dangerous idea that mental illness does not exist and that mental issues can be treated alone through spiritual discipline.

There is a popular Christian movement among preachers called "The Sufficiency of Scripture." Of course, we as Christians believe this. Sometimes, however, some faith leaders will take this to an extreme by believing illnesses causing a broken mind can be cured with Scripture alone. I wonder if they would also apply this same line of reasoning to a broken leg.

There were well-meaning Christian friends, when the doctor found Ron's eye cancer, who advised us to please not let the doctors remove his eye. We were instead to pray and trust that God would cast out the devil from his eye. From what we were told by the doctors, if they had not physically removed the cancer, he would not be with us today. Certainly, the Patch the Pirate ministry would never have been born.

I cannot imagine the depths of hopelessness an unbeliever who deals with mental illness must feel without Christ in their life. This life is all they have. Even a believer in Christ who is in clinical depression can still experience hopelessness in his heart. Our Jonathan, apart from medicine to improve the misfiring of his neurotransmitters causing depression when not on proper medicine, did not feel any love or hope. When on his needed meds, however, imparting God's wisdom to him gave spiritual support as well as the physical.

I seek not to cast blame or point fingers, though I have wanted to at times. I seek to share the perspective of someone who has walked the pathways and lived the trial, one who has heard the theories and experimented with the treatments, and one who has seen the outcomes. I seek to give caution to the counselor, empathy to the caregiver, and help for the hurting.

Important for biblical counselors to remember is this: Suicide is often the result of an untreated mental health condition.[21]

Over ninety percent of people who die by suicide have an untreated mental illness at the time of death.

I must also insert the unfortunate fact that there are those who found a medicine to help at the beginning of the illness, but went off and then tried going back without success with the same medicine. When a medicine is helping a mental condition, the person taking it should never go off without a physician's advice.

Fortunately, there are many success stories for those with mental illness. I should insert, most success stories experience challenges along the way, but an abundance of patience has been administered. Success stories share four attributes:

1. Doctors keep a close watch on the patient's medicine(s).

2. The patient takes them faithfully.

3. The patient has a strong support group.

4. The patient receives Christian teaching, counseling, and community from their church.

---

[21]https://www.nami.org/get-involved/awareness-events/suicide-prevention-awareness-month

Look Up, There Is Hope—

Help for the Mental Health Sufferer

May 2020

If you are struggling with some type of depression, this chapter is for you.

I am very aware that if you are in the midst of depression or schizophrenia, the words on the pages of this book will probably not reach your eyes. And if you have come out of your depression, you will feel no need to read it. I am driven, however, to make an effort.

First of all, look up.

> *I will lift up mine eyes unto the hills, from whence cometh my help. My help cometh from the LORD, which made heaven and earth. (Psalm 121:1–2)*

Secondly, there is hope. Hope is more than a nice thought. I realize that you may be so far down in your deep, dark hole, that you cannot see any light. You have to trust; *there is light where you cannot see. There is hope where you cannot feel.*

> *Who among you fears the LORD and obeys the word of his servant? Let him who walks in the darkness and has no light trust in the name of the LORD and rely on his God. (Isaiah 50:10)*

Even if you presently are not feeling any love, the fact remains that there is love. You are loved by God, you are loved by many who have walked your road before, you are loved by family and friends, and you are loved by me.

As fathers, even grandfathers, want to hold their children in their arms to comfort them, our Heavenly Father desires to hold His children in His arms when they are in need of sympathy. I love the symbolic picture of two sets of footprints walking in the sand, depicting that God holds our hand as we walk down this journey called life. All of a sudden you see only one set of footprints in the sand.

Did God forsake me?

No—never! When we can no longer walk holding God's hand, He then lifts us up and carries us. Whether limp and lifeless or whether kicking and screaming, He patiently and lovingly sustains us.

Although you may feel alone, make sure you physically are not. If you live by yourself, may I suggest you move to a home where there is someone who loves and cares about you. If you cannot, call NAMI (National Association of Mental Illness) and see if there is a home in your area where you can live with people who will be a support to you. Or you can rent an apartment that is part of someone else's home.

You are never walking alone. Though your eyes can't see, there is a whole community out there that shares your same burdens, fears, and mental health struggles. You need support. We all need support, especially when we are so weak and trodden down that we cannot pull ourselves up without help. There is no disgrace in reaching out for help. We all have, at various points of need in our lives.

- You need medical support. Know there are thousands helped daily with psychiatric medicines.

- You need spiritual support. Find a biblical counselor in your area.

- You need emotional support. If possible, live with someone who cares about you.

If you are in a place of despair, please allow those who love you to be there for you. Sometimes it is difficult to find the right support you need, but it exists. Allow yourself to grab on to the rope of any help extended to you. You are worthy. Your life is worthy.

Please seek help from a doctor familiar with your illness. Doctors exist in most every city who specialize in treating people with mental illness. These very dear persons are called psychiatrists. Perform due diligence when selecting yours. A Christian psychiatrist is best, if you can locate one.

Biblical counselors are very helpful. If you indeed have an organic illness, these godly people will be there for you after a doctor gives you medical intervention. Otherwise, counseling alone may help briefly but is best when coupled with medical help.

Medicine is not a bad thing. Many people are on heart medicine, blood pressure medicine, diabetes medicine, chemotherapy treatments, and many are on medicines that help the mind. There is nothing shameful about it. As others have been helped with medicine, I pray that you will give opportunity to be helped likewise. I am personally on an antidepressant and am able to function better with its assistance.

I have assimilated a list of what I hope to be helpful tips for you:

- Be patient.

- Listen to biblical teaching podcasts.

- Pray.

- Get help from a professional doctor, preferably a psychiatrist, who understands what you are going through.

- When prescribed meds, take them. It might take a little time to find the right one or combination. Hang in there, it's worth it. And please, never go off any medicine without a doctor's advice. Ninety percent of suicides are those who have untreated mental illness.

- Realize it may take several years to find your right medicine(s). And once you find one that helps, it's not a straight road to healing. The road may go up and down, left and right, before plateauing.

- There are many who have walked your same path and are living meaningful lives.

- Realize that you have a new norm. It's okay. You may have a few limitations, but everyone does.

- Pray.

- Be conscious of helping those with whom you live in any physical way you can—take out the trash, clean your room, help cook, help clean, do your own laundry, and so forth.

- Be aware that some won't understand your illness. Don't worry what others think. The fact is, many do understand. For certain, God understands.

- Please never give in to a temptation to take your life. By doing so, you will devastate your family members and friends for the rest of their lives. There is always hope for you to get better.

- Pray.

- Strengthen your spiritual, emotional, and physical muscles. You are more than likely in this for the long haul. You can do it! Get exercise. Get sunshine. Get vitamin D. Get magnesium. Get valerian root. Do whatever your caregiver, counselor, and doctor tell you to do.

- Seek out an integrative physician. Hormone imbalance, thyroid issues, anemia, Lyme's disease, an infection, and so forth may be at the root or at least part of your problem.

- Accept that God is allowing what you are going through. Love and trust Him. He is glorified when you trust Him, especially when journeying through trials. He will ultimately work your trial out for good.

- Focus on every blessing you have, no matter how great or how small.

We as human beings all need *hope*. Life without hope is no life at all. God created you with a divine purpose for your life.

> *Now the hope of God fill you with all joy and peace in believing, that ye may abound in hope, through the power of the Holy Ghost. (Romans 15:13)*

We have no greater reason for hope than that of eternal life in an awesome place especially prepared for believers in Christ. This place will be free of sorrow, sickness, death, and pain.

I know things may at times look bleak for you, but call the darkness what it is: it began in the Garden of Eden—the result of Satan's lies. Remember, Satan is the author of depression. He wants you to believe depression exists because God is not good, but it is instead because Satan is evil.

Before you can heal spiritually, you need to trust God and believe in His goodness. If you blame God for your illness, you will not only be in depression, but filled with bitterness. Even when your eyes can't see, know this truth: God is good. Please look up. There is hope, and you are worth it.

"I'm on Assignment"—
Help for the Caregiver

May 2020

I believe we are all born caregivers.

- Parents bring a child into the world and become its caregiver. Some children are born with special needs that constitute extra-loving caregiving.

- When children leave the home and get married, they become caregivers of their own children; even a child who never has children may become a caregiver of students, friends, or family.

- The original parents now have grandchildren, becoming partial caregivers, and if the need arises, full-time caregivers.

- Then there sometimes comes the day when one parent may need to become the caregiver of their spouse.

- At the end, the children often become caregivers of their parents. The cycle is thus completed, and it begins all over again.

We should all learn to be cheerful, contented caregivers—the type we hope to have one day. If you are in a tough situation as a caregiver, remember the chorus of a song Ron wrote for children:

> *Little by little, inch by inch,*
> *By the yard it's hard, by the inch, what a cinch!*
> *Never stare up the stairs, just step up the steps.*
> *Little by little, inch by inch.*

Repeating to myself, "I'm on assignment," has become extremely helpful for me. God gives us different assignments as we travel through our seasons of life. It's all good. During our assignments, God remains present to lift us up, hold our hand, cheer us on, all the while knowing that through the assignment, we will be more knowledgeable and better equipped for caregiving.

After Jon became ill, I had trouble sleeping for months on end. I counted sheep, quoted Scripture, prayed, and listened to sacred music to no effect of catapulting me into much-needed slumber. I was exhausted. I also experienced days I could not make myself get off the couch. I was truly experiencing asthenia, the first "A" of depression—muscle weakness and flu-like symptoms.

At times, all I could do was rest. I felt like a bum and a couch potato. I truly tried to trust in God to the best of my ability, but the trauma of Jon's illness was more than my body was handling. Dealing with the beginnings of Ron's frontotemporal dementia, made matters worse.

I unashamedly admit to having gone off and on an antidepressant and sleeping pills for the last twenty plus years. I have had time durations that I did okay without either and times when I needed both. I have tried several times going off the sleeping pills. I can get pretty crabby after missing much sleep. Each time I tried to go off the pills, Ron recommended I go back on. Presently I am on both. If God sends a rowboat to rescue you from drowning, get in.

I understand that some doctors give out antidepressants like candy. Although I don't question this, I personally have not seen it. I did have one friend several weeks ago say they were appalled that their doctor suggested they might go on one. Additionally, I hear there are people who take and are addicted to medicines that they don't need, which is, of course, not good. However, the people I know on psychiatric medicines indeed need them.

After our son Jonathan died, someone gave me a carved wooden cross that fits very nicely into the hand. I keep this cross on my desk and hold it frequently to remind me of Him whom I trust. If my heart starts racing, I breathe slowly and deeply, hold onto my cross, and my heartbeat noticeably slows down.

There are days when the "caree" (the one being cared for) in your home does not want to leave his room or even say hello. As a caregiver (the one who cares for the caree), you have to realize it is just one of those days. It's okay. There is a hard line between being authoritative with a caree to do something you know is good for them and being harsh in the process, speaking to them in a vengeful or demeaning way. I have found that when my caree was in an episode, it was best to remain silent, capitulate, and wait for a better time. Always important was to speak respectfully.

I learned that when Jonathan was not well and in an agitated state of mind, I would say, "Not today, Devil. You are going beneath my feet." I opened the door and kicked the Devil out of my house. Some days as the caregiver, you have to stay in a constant state of prayer to keep the Devil out. He wants to defeat and destroy you and your family.

If your caree reacts to you in anger, you have to be determined not to take offense and actively practice forgiveness. I learned to just remain calm and quiet. Jon would eventually settle down and most times later ask for forgiveness.

Mental illness is called the disease that doesn't get a casserole. You know when you get cancer, people bring you casseroles. When you get mental illness, you many times get nothing. People don't know what to say or do.

I don't blame or judge anyone who feels they cannot deal with someone in their home who is mentally or emotionally unwell. When you think, "I cannot handle this," remember "God can." As a caregiver, it's all you can do at times to keep your own sanity—almost like experiencing a bomb going off in your living room every day. You don't know the exact time, but you are certain of its occurrence.

If you have an opportunity for an alternative place that will take care of your loved one, consider taking it! The situation resulting from being a caregiver for dementia or mental illness can be exhausting. It demands ultimate patience, gentleness, kindness, and the love of Christ for both the caree and the caregiver. The fruits of the spirit will be tested. "Dear Jesus, You are the teacher. Hallelujah!"

Let me mention that you will probably get much well-meaning advice from observing family members and close friends about how to handle your caree. Sometimes you have to take it with a grain of salt. No one knows fully until they have walked in your shoes. Pray for God's help and wisdom and do the best you can. This is all that God asks of you and of me.

Pain has no comma and no color. Pain has no comma or moment of rest, because we gain strength from one pain, only to prepare for the next. And pain has no color because it affects us all—black, white, and brown. As we go through pain, we become advocates of that pain.

The caregiver needs to find ways to cope and take care of himself or herself. The caregiver needs spiritual feeding from above and from the Word of God. The caregiver needs some time off and ways to relax and have fun.

As a caregiver, because you are on assignment, here are a few tips I have found helpful for me.

- Love the suffering individual unconditionally. God loves us when we are not at our best.

- Pray.

- Be patient. God is teaching you invaluable lessons you can learn no other way.

- Make sure your caree gets regular checkups with a doctor. If at all possible, don't send your caree to the doctor alone. It is likely they do not believe they need help. Their perspective may be askew, so the doctor needs your perspective.

- Don't be dismayed if your caree won't let you go with them to the doctor. Hopefully, they are at least going. If they continually refuse to go, you may have to go by yourself and discover your options. It may take several tries before finding the right doctor for your loved one.

- Keep repeating to yourself, "I'm on assignment."

- Make sure your caree takes his medicine. Understand that it usually takes a while to find the correct medicine or combo of them. Your caree may get worse at first. Keep a close eye on him whenever starting a new medicine.

- Go to a support group if you can; they are out there. NAMI (National Affiliation of Mental Illness) is very beneficial.

- Repeat again, "I'm on assignment," and pray.

- Make your pastor aware of your situation. If he doesn't understand, I would try to find a different one. You need spiritual support from a spiritual leader!

- If your caree will not get help and is a danger to you, you may need to call the police. They should be able to give you advice. Don't put yourself and other loved ones in peril.

- If needed, you may have to get your loved one committed to a mental institution. This is always the very last resort. If precious time has gone by, and your caree refuses to get help or go on medicine and becomes a danger to you or theirself, going to the hospital may be your only recourse. It is traumatic, but unfortunately, sometimes necessary.

- If there is any way to find laughter, it will help you and your caree. Ron and Jonathan watched a lot of *Andy Griffith* and *I Love Lucy* shows.

- Do all you can for your loved one. Family members should be our dearest people on earth. If we are called to love our *neighbor* as *ourselves*, there is no *neighbor* so close as a family member. Remember, the tables could be turned. How would you want to be understood and cared for?

- If you know that your caree needs help and the doctor you take them to cannot see it, get a second opinion.

- If your caree will be willing, take them to a holistic doctor. Sometimes getting needed hormones, thyroid supplements, or vitamins, specifically Vitamin D and magnesium, can be helpful.

- Trust and pray.

- Try to get your caree outdoors in the fresh air, just to sit or even better, to walk. The vitamin D from the sun is very good for depression, and exercise increases serotonin and dopamine, the "happy hormones." Serotonin is found in the brain, gut, and blood platelets.

- Repeat, "I'm on assignment."

- Try to leave your emotions out when your caree is not in a good state of mind. More than likely, when he is not well, he will say things to you that are "out-of-the-ordinary" unkind. Remember, it is the disease talking. It is better to remain silent than to retaliate. Answering in anger will only escalate the situation. Sometimes you may need to bite your tongue.

- Always choose your words very carefully when speaking with your caree. Remember, facial expressions and tone of voice speak louder than words. But when words are necessary, choose adjectives that are positive rather than negative. This advice is to the benefit of you both.

- Trust and pray.

- You set the temperature of the home. Do it to the best of your ability. You want to live in peace as much as possible. The ball is mostly in your court, as you cannot control the other court.

- Find ways to get private time for yourself to rejuvenate.

- If your caree feels up to it, do special things with them that you know they will enjoy. Try going shopping. Drive around your city. Get a coffee together. Go to the zoo. Go for a walk at the park and throw a frisbee.

- You are not only caregiver, but cheerleader. Oxytocin, secreted by the pituitary gland, is known as the "cuddle hormone" or the "love hormone." This is the hormone cheerleaders give and helps to convey the sense of belonging. It is known to have a positive impact on mood and emotions. Make sure your caree gets "cheerleading" from you.

We have the gift of life only because God wills it. You and I will not rise up yesterday, today, or tomorrow without the permission and power of God. We are on an incredible journey called life where we encounter many twists and turns. Sometimes a twist in our journey surprises us with joy, yet at another with sorrow.

We have only the dashboard view—a very limited visibility on our journey. God has the helicopter view. He knows exactly where each earthly journey is going to begin, its length, its bumps and curves, and where it ultimately is going to end. I cannot help but think often of Jon's struggle and his early death; in fact, I am reminded of them daily. But I choose to believe that all struggle is eclipsed by the glorious reality of a powerful God, my loving Savior, and what He can do.

My prayer is that you will see these truths in your own context: the depth of your own struggle and the chaos in the world around you. The end of the story, however, for every believer is the same—mountains moved, the victory won, the struggle overcome—not because of the greatness of our faith but because of the greatness of God.

The verse "the just shall live by faith" (Romans 1:17) is one of the most powerful messages in Scripture and has become my verse to live by. I sent this Scripture along with one of Jon's unpublished tunes to our friend Chris Anderson. I also sent devotionals I have written on this Scripture so Chris can see why it has come to mean so much to me.

Chris took my thoughts, added his own, and created a beautiful text that expresses exactly what I wanted said. I am so thankful to Chris Anderson for giving these truths beautiful flight. We pray that this song will lead you in affirming these truths with us.

The Just Shall Live by Faith
Lyrics: Chris Anderson;
Music: Jonathan Hamilton © 2020 by Majesty Music, Inc.

In the Word I read of a mustard seed—
Faith is small, but God is great.
My reliance lies not on me, but Christ:
The just shall live by faith.

Refrain

Lord, I believe Your promise—I will trust in You!
Help my unbelief!
Though my grip is frail, Yours will never fail:
The just shall live by faith.

In my flesh I see nothing good in me—
Only pride, and fear, and hate.
My eternal hope rests in Christ alone:
The just shall live by faith.

In my grief I brood, lost in solitude—
Yet I pray, I trust, I wait.
I'll endure the night, sure of endless light:
The just shall live by faith.

Dealing with Grips of Grief

May 12, 2021 (eight years to the day after Jon's death)

Morning Minutes

The losses are His way of accomplishing the gains.[22]
—*Elisabeth Elliot*

I have had eight years now to live through the loss of our son. Jonathan's suicide was not Ron's or my fault, nor was it his doctor's, although I have many times blamed myself. We all wish we had done some things differently and possibly prevented Jon's death from occurring. Dr. Craddock and his entire team are not to blame, but were a tremendous source of blessing, encouragement, and physical help for our Jonathan.

This seems to be a good place to give a shout out to Dr. Craddock's assistant, Sandra Hamilton and her husband Kim, a Christian counselor. Many thanks to you both for your love and caring for our Jonathan.

---

[22]Elisabeth Elliot, *Finding Your Way Through Loneliness* (Ada, MI: Revel, 2011), 70.

Kim counsels many parents whose children have committed suicide. He writes to me a beautiful message after previewing this book:

> *I've found with grief like many things, we either get stuck on the side of trying to hold on to the pain or we choose to focus on the cherished memories. Jon has so many of both. I have noted a pattern of his constant desire to be released from all that was troubling. When he talked with you and Ron, he'd find some relief. . . . The Lord made us for connection and communication. . . . In communicating, it connects us and lets us know we're not alone . . . As the words pour out of you as you write this book, you're probably realizing how much you had bottled up. God is now giving you the courage, the release, and the love to pour into words to help someone who feels so alone. . . . At the end of this time of reflection, I pray that you see that love is what is compelling you . . . for Jon, for Ron, for all your kids, and that love is what is pushing you through this.*
>
> *The Lord loves you and is catching every tear and guiding each keystroke as you share Jon's story. . . . So many struggle at first with a child that has committed suicide and the feeling of why they could not have protected them, . . . but reality sets in and their child is now home and no longer suffering from the deception of the evil one. No one could have prevented or delayed or even changed in that moment what occurred.*
>
> *God allowed what was bad to occur to release Jon from that chaos. He turned that moment into good. Your faith is your sustenance and your window into being eternal in your soul. Smile in knowing that the journey has hardly begun with your son . . . and how this part of the story is just the foreword for so many chapters to come.*

How have I learned to deal with the grips of grief?

I have done multiple renovations in the different homes in which we have lived. With demolition comes dust and debris. I am presently adding a handicapped bathroom for my husband Ron as his dementia is progressing. Adding this room has required cutting through a concrete wall in order to make a door entrance for access to his bedroom. Concrete dust particles were not only thick in the work area but seeped into the entire house.

The renovation process reminds me of dealing with grief. Grief is real. Grief is the loss of something or someone that creates a hole in your heart. The grips of grief reach deep into your very soul. The cutting of the hole in your heart is like the cutting through that concrete block to make a door. Grief overtakes your being like debris overtakes your home. You can clean up the main debris, taking hours and hours of work, but you will keep finding remnants of it here and there. As time goes on, not as much will be present. But when you least expect it, you will find some under a book or behind a picture frame.

When dealing with grief, the most debris occurs when the hole is cut into your heart. You clean it up as best you can by trusting God, reading Scripture, and believing God is always, only good. This process sometimes takes days, months, and even years. Much later, you can find hidden remnants of the grief here and there. And when you least expect it, one kind word about your loved one from a friend or any reminder of your loss, will bring the grief right back into your heart.

Losing our precious son Jonathan on Mother's Day is similar. I have been dealing with the grips of grief as time passes, trusting in God's goodness, and reading Scripture. I have a peace in my heart and joy in my spirit that Jonathan is with the Lord. Still, a few kind words from friends on subsequent Mother's Days make tears flow. I will never completely be over the grief of losing our son, but I believe with all my heart that God is in control and taking care of him in a better place.

God is our Divine Builder. If we allow Him, He will use the grief to renovate our hearts.

I know I will never in this life get completely over the grief of losing our son Jonathan. Unfortunately, grief will not be denied. I am still sad I never got to say, "Goodbye." But how could I have ever done that?

But this does not lessen the confidence in my heart that God is good. I've learned to saturate myself with Scripture for survival. Each trial becomes a treasure and brings with its external pain, eternal gain. We all will know rejoicing beyond measure when we have the privilege of laying these treasures at His feet.

My husband Ron's dementia has been a slow-moving grief. I know the outcome of his disease and watch his decline over time. I haven't felt his loss yet; that will be another cut in the concrete. The door, however, made into the living space of my life will lead me into a new room God has prepared for me. As in physical renovation, there is also beauty beyond the dust in God's spiritual renovation.

Marty Hamilton Nelson, Ron's sister, has what is called Meniere's disease. Meniere's is named after its founder and is a balance and hearing disorder that affects the inner ear. The disease may go into remission, but it is chronic.

When Marty is affected by the disease, the world seems to swim around her. She doesn't know which way is up and which is down. What seems to help during these attacks is for her to find something stable to place one of her hands on. It needs to be something immoveable to which she can place her confidence. Because her inner in-balance is all askew, a steady and constant object helps her realize what is true and what is not.

When we are lopsided emotionally, physically, and spiritually due to the loss of something or someone dear to us, placing our hand in the hand of the One who is immoveable and constant can help us regain our balance. When the world seems to swim around inside of us, placing our faith in the unchangeable God can steady us.

We as humans have a disease: sin and lack of trust. Our disease may go into remission, but it is chronic.

> *And straightway the father of the child cried out, and said with tears, Lord, I believe: help thou mine unbelief. (Mark 9:24)*

The Apostle Paul tells us:

> *Therefore, my beloved brethren, be ye stedfast, unmoveable, always abounding in the work of the Lord. (1 Corinthians 15:58)*

How do we become immovable spiritually? By placing our hand not on an object like a table, but better yet on a person—our rooted Heavenly Father.

> *Know therefore that the LORD thy God, he is God, the faithful God, which keepeth covenant and mercy with them that love him and keep his commandments to a thousand generations. (Deuteronomy 7:9)*

> *Now unto the King eternal, immortal, invisible, the only God, be honour and glory forever and forever. Amen. (1 Timothy 1:17)*

Dr. Steve Hankins, seminary professor and friend, says, "We learn through the life of Jeremiah the speaking of the Lord during a tragic time of divine judgment and chastening because of Israel's sin."

> *Remember my affliction and my wandering, the wormwood and bitterness. Surely my soul remembers and is bowed down within me. This I recall to my mind, therefore I have hope. The LORD's lovingkindnesses indeed never cease, for His compassions never fail. They are new every morning, Great is Your faithfulness. (Lamentations 3:19–23)*

I am reminded of Joseph's loss of his home, his father, and the betrayal he experienced by his brothers. Joseph became the savior of not only his family, but of all Israel through and because of his grief. God exalted him to second ruler over Egypt under Pharoah himself. Joseph trusted God and was able to have such a deep conviction in his heart that he was able to declare at the end of his life, "But as for you, ye thought evil against me; but God meant it unto good, to bring to pass, as it is this day, to save much people alive" (Genesis 50:20).

When we think of suffering in the Bible, our thoughts immediately go to the character Job. I wonder how many books, poems, sermons, and word-of-mouth lessons have been shared down through the ages about the life of one just man. Some receive thorns like Paul. Some receive thorn packages like Job.

> *Suffering is a fraternity.*
> *Not everyone joins.*
> *It's not an easy induction.*
> *An invite doesn't come in the mail.*
> *The membership is by word of mouth.*
> *There is no sign out for this one.*
> *—Pastor Doug Fisher*

So much transpires in Job chapter one. Job is the man Scripture tells us fears God with reverential trust, and he deliberately avoids and abstains from evil. This perfect and upright man has seven sons and three daughters with wealth so great that he is the most powerful man in all of the east (v. 1–3).

We learn that Job loves his children so much that he rises up early and offers burnt sacrifices for each of them to be certain that if they are delinquent in their own sacrifices, their sins will be covered (v. 5).

Satan enters the halls of heaven and comes before God's throne accusing Job of only being upright because of the hedge of protection placed around him and because of how abundantly blessed he is. Satan continues, "But put forth thine hand now, and touch all that he hath, and he will curse thee to thy face" (v. 11). God responds, "Behold, all that he hath is in thy power; only upon himself put not forth thine hand" (v. 12).

Due to God's permission, Satan is unleashed. Within the next ten verses, Job loses his livestock, his servants, his house, and even his sons and daughters. Unbelievably, all of this transpires in ten short verses (vv. 13–22).

In chapter two, Satan comes before God's throne the second time. I can imagine Satan a little perturbed because after all Job has lost, he is still holding fast to his integrity. But Satan reasons, if God will only allow Job's health to be attacked, then Job will denounce his God. Satan does not realize the strength of this God-fearing man. God gives permission for Satan to attack Job's body, but to not let him die. Job becomes covered with sore boils from his head to his feet. Afterwards he is taunted by his own wife to "curse God and die" (v. 9).

Next on the scene enter Job's three friends—Eliphaz, Bildad, and Zophar. Upon hearing of all the hardships Job has faced, they come and sit quietly by him for seven days and seven nights to be a support while he grieves. They say nothing but are just there as a support, which is a lesson to us as we help others grieve.

On day eight, in chapter three, Job breaks the silence. In verses 1–24 he verbalizes his grief and rues the day he was born. In Job 3:25 we learn something interesting about Job. "For the thing which I greatly feared is come upon me, and that which I was afraid of is come unto me." I can't help but think that perhaps the thing which Job feared most was losing his children. Very unfortunately, this comes to pass. Do you remember in Job 1:5 that Job offered burnt sacrifices early every morning for his children to make sure they hadn't been delinquent in following God's command?

Job 4:3–4 tells us another important fact about Job. Eliaphaz, Job's friend says to him, "Behold, thou hast instructed many, and thou hast strengthened the weak hands. Thy words have upholden him that was falling, and thou hast strengthened the feeble knees." Job is a teacher! I didn't remember this about Job in my previous readings. Job is not only a teacher but also an encourager. I love this about him.

Job chapters 4–37 is an elongated and detailed discourse between Job and his friends. The three supporting friends break silence and unjustly accuse Job of being responsible for all his tragedies and maladies. You can't help but think, "With friends like this, who needs enemies?" As I skim through the discourse, I would love to someday go back and do a study of what all is said between the four friends. I'm sure it will prove to be very interesting.

It should be noted that there is no time frame indicated from Job chapter 4 through chapter 42. Job's depression could have carried on for years.

We come to the conclusion of our story in chapters 38–42. God breaks His silence and speaks to Job. "Where wast thou when I laid the foundations of the earth? . . . Who shut up the seas with doors? . . . Hast thou given the horse strength?" (Job 38:4, 8, 19). I don't believe that God is reprimanding Job, but reminding him that He, God, was and is and will always be in control.

Job 40:3–4 says, "Then Job answered the LORD, and said, Behold, I am vile; what shall I answer thee? I will lay mine hand upon my mouth." Job 42:1–2 and 6 says, "Then Job answered the LORD, and said, I know that thou canst do every thing, and that no thought can be withholden from thee. . . . Wherefore I abhor myself, and repent in dust and ashes." This is exactly where Job needs to be—broken so God can use him.

Chapter 42 of the book of Job is my favorite!

First, God wraps up the loose ends regarding Job's friends. They are by no means going to be let off the hook for their judgmental spirits and for the bad advice they gave Job when he was at his lowest. Job 42:7 declares that "the LORD said to Eliphaz . . . My wrath is kindled against thee, and against thy two friends: for ye have not spoken of me the thing that is right, as my servant Job hath." God instructs the friends to offer burnt offerings before Job, "and Job will pray for you: for him will I accept" (v. 8). I believe it very possible that after Job's three friends confessed to one another, they became closer friends with Job than they had been before.

Secondly, in Job 42:10, after Job prayed for his friends, God "turned the captivity of Job" and "also gave Job twice as much as he had before." Job's wealth was doubled, and he is given seven more sons and three more daughters. God did, as God does. He turned bad into good, loss into blessing, a prison into a pulpit. Verse 11 tells us, "Then came there unto him all his brethren, and all his sisters, and all they that had been of his acquaintance before, and did eat bread with him in his house: and they bemoaned him, and comforted him over all the evil that the LORD had brought upon him." Verse 12 says, "So the LORD blessed the latter end of Job more than his beginning."

Thirdly, more than the wealth and children for which Job is blessed, God increases Job's influence. In chapter 4 we learn that Job is a teacher and an encourager. Can we think of anyone else besides Christ who has taught us more and encouraged us more than Job through his sufferings? But first, Job had to be brought closer to God as only is accomplished through suffering and humility. Job passed the test and remained upright. Then, and only then, was God able to multiply Job's influence.

Count it all blessing when you are counted among the righteous to enter the suffering fraternity with Job.

One of the best ways to counter grief is with praise. There is great power in praise.

Joni Earickson Tada, Christian author and singer, became a quadriplegic from a diving accident when she was very young. I heard her say once that sleeping at night was very difficult. If she wanted to turn over, she couldn't. If she had an itch on her face, she couldn't scratch it. She would lie in her bed for hours unable to sleep and miserable.

So, when her helpers arrived in the morning to get her up and dressed for the day, their first order of business was to sing a hymn together. This action literally "pulled her spirit up by the heartstrings" and got her ready to face the day. If Joni Tada, paralyzed from the neck down for decades, can have her spirit lifted up with praise, so can those in the grips of grief.

The emotional loss of a child must be similar to the physical loss of a limb. When it happens, the pain is excruciating. After the event is past, you still from time to time relive the agony. You think you have overcome, but when you least expect it, something or someone will elicit the ugly memory, causing a meltdown. Unexpected meltdowns become expected.

Over time the scars heal, but you live the rest of your earthly life handicapped, in full realization of the depth of your loss and its effects. You learn to compensate for what you are missing and hopefully will be accepting and not become bitter. Bitterness plus a devastating loss must be a terrible place to exist. I refuse to live there. I choose to exist in the immensity and fullness of God's love. Through the toughest of times, God's goodness is there for all of us.

Songs in the Night

To deliver our children by natural childbirth, Ron and I were taught through Lamaze classes the principle of finding a focal point. During the most intense part of the labor, the twenty minutes or so of transition before the baby is born, it helps to find a focal point near you on which to place your attention.

After four deliveries, and while delivering our son Jason, I discovered an even better focusing tactic: instead of focusing on an inanimate object, I focused on a part of my body that didn't hurt. During Jason's delivery, I focused on my arm, saying to myself, "O my arm feels so good. Ahhh! It feels wonderful. It doesn't hurt at all." This practice really helped. I wish I had thought of it earlier—1979 when Jon was born, to be exact.

The art of focusing on blessings helps carry us through everyday life. We must learn to practice to near perfection the art of focusing on our blessings, not the things that hurt! This art is very similar to having a focal point in childbearing. Sometimes pain is so intense, focusing on anything else is unreasonable and impossible. If we practice the art most of the time, however, it will come to be more a part of us.

I indeed have blessings abundant on which to focus:

- a blest ministry of creating music for fellow Christians to glorify God

- numerous songs my husband has written that continue to minister to me and others

- five incredible children: Jonathan, Tara, Alyssa, Megan, Jason

- two fabulous sons-in-love—Ben Farrell, who is a magnificent preacher and pastor and has a gorgeous singing voice, and Adam Morgan, who is brilliant and funny and a lawyer who has become a fabulous songwriter and Patch story writer. Adam is also a South Carolina State House Representative

- our daughter Tara is a homemaker, pastor's wife, and has given us two grandchildren, Clayton and Chloe; Tara is a talented pianist and vocalist

- our daughter Megan and her husband Adam have decided to come on-board and manage Majesty Music and Patch the Pirate; they are continuing the ministry—writing all the new stories and songs; they have given us two grandchildren Ella Marie and Hamilton Michael

- our daughter Alyssa has become my right arm in helping me care for Ron with his dementia; Alyssa and I have also done a duo piano book and recording together

- our son Jason is the youngest—a guitarist, soloist, and on fire serving God with his talents. He was a music pastor in Wisconsin but is presently furthering his education in voice performance

- Alyssa, Ron, and I live in a cozy, mountain cottage for which I was able to design a complete makeover

I am in a good place, the center of God's will for me.

There is no greater joy than that which follows great sorrow.

We can't even begin to imagine the joy awaiting us when we see our loved ones in heaven.

If you've never been in the valley, you cannot truly appreciate the mountaintop.

If there were never the rain, there would never be the rainbow.

Cara Davis, mentioned earlier as one of Jon's close friends, messaged me just several days after I was finishing writing the first draft of this book.

> *Jonathan is one of the most special people I've ever had the pleasure of knowing, and I fully intend to give him a giant hug when we meet again one day. . . . Literally, the majority of my childhood memories include your sweet family and to this day bring me such joy.*

George Clements, Jonathan's best friend during his adult years, sends me a beautiful floral arrangement with pink roses every Mother's Day. Let me repeat—George is a gem.

After Jonathan's death, James and Thelma Scott, who took Jonathan in at the Shenandoah Boys' Ranch, sent us beautiful outdoor chimes that we keep on our back porch. Engraved on a wooden circle attached to the chimes is: "In loving memory of Jonathan C. Hamilton and his love for God's gift of music." When I hear the chimes, I think of Jonathan singing with the angels in heaven.

One of my biggest blessings is the joy I receive from our family making sacred music recordings together. Even though Ron and Jonathan cannot presently sing with us, they are both a part of us with the music they have written.

I am so grateful to God for giving Jonathan musical talent. Jonathan's legacy lives on through the beautiful songs he wrote in the darkness:

Higher Ground • Lift Him Up • The Secret Place • The Shadow of the Cross • Rock of Ages • I Will Go • I Am Weak, but You Are Strong • Shepherd of My Soul • You Are Always Good • O the Goodness of the Lord • and most recently, The Just Shall Live by Faith

Ironically, Jonathan is literally on the higher ground of which he wrote.

I also can never underestimate the blessing my husband's music and Patch the Pirate ministry has been on our entire family's life. What started in 1978, lives on today. Forty-three recordings later, we never in our wildest dreams could have planned such a ministry. It is definitely not our doing. God has other objectives, however, and turns tragedy into triumph. Only a good God can do such a marvelous thing.

God gives Ron a forty-year window to grow the kingdom of God through the writing of beautiful melodies and lyrics. The very gift of language God gave Ron for forty years has now been taken from him by frontotemporal dementia. This has been God's plan, and I stand by and rest in that.

Ron and I have said many times to each other, "What better way to teach children God's truths than through music?"—another reminder to me that God is omniscient and has a plan.

God is giving me numerous opportunities to share Jonathan's story. After giving Jonathan's testimony at a church in Illinois, a psychiatric nurse came up to me afterwards and told me what another nurse had communicated to me previously, "Do you know what I got most out of your story? Your son was very lucky to have you and Ron as parents who stuck by him and gave him love and support." I choked back tears and have never forgotten what she told me.

Love and support may be the greatest thing you can do for your loved one as well.

Thank you, God, for giving Jon songs in the darkness and us the strength to take care of our son.

Last Thoughts

My friend and spiritual mentor, Sarah Bennett, has advised me as I have written this book:

Keep giving glory to God, and He will pour out the words from your heart to the page.

I believe God has truly poured out the words for me.

As time has gone by since Jon's death, I have tried my best not to dwell on all that has transpired, much less write about it. After the funeral, I buried myself in my existing family and my work at Majesty Music. I have feared that the more time passed, I would not recall much of what had happened regarding Jon's sickness. But uncannily, as I have written, God has brought back to my mind so many details that I had forgotten. I have prayed that He would only bring to mind what He wanted me to share.

Oran Bell, Sarah Bennett's dad and Grandma Bell's husband, had a Haitian man who followed him all over Haiti, carrying his bags and doing whatever was needed. His name was Louis. Grandma Bell told Louis, "When you get to heaven, you can hire Oran to carry your crowns." When I told Sarah today how much she has influenced me spiritually, she said (tongue in cheek), "When we both get to heaven, I can hire you to carry around my crowns as far as to Jesus' feet."

October 27, 2020

Some of this chapter will be repetitious but are things I believe worth reiterating.

I had an aha moment yesterday, October 27. Someone called me with an urgent prayer request. This person became emotional on the phone, and the sadness broke my heart. I asked God, "Why are there so many trials on this earth?" Then almost immediately in the next breath I thought, "Of course. Trials are the transits that keep our brain currents connected to our Creator and ever mindful of our eternal purpose."

I think of my own life. When I personally am not going through a trial or a hardship, I tend to get caught up in worldly affairs, fun times, luxuries, and comforts. I forget that the *here and now* only serves to prepare me for the *there and then*. We are not for this world, but for the world to come. God is continuing Jon's story in His own will and way.

Oftentimes it takes trials to cause me to more intently focus on God, lean on Him more, pray more, and more fervently reach out to others to share the good news of salvation. If I always lived a life of ease, I am certain I wouldn't feel the need to focus on eternity and on the real purpose of this life. Without a doubt, *I know God best* when I have to cling to Him.

I think of Ron's life. If only he could be with me in mind as I write this book. This story is as much about him as anyone else. I can only pray he would be accepting and proud of the writing on these pages. I do know he was our family's solid rock through Jonathan's illness. Dementia, however, has taken its course.

Two convictions I have come to believe that we must firmly believe with all our heart.

1. God is always, only good.

2. The just shall live by faith.

When I prayed in 1978 that Ron wouldn't lose his eye, was God not good because he answered my prayer differently than I wanted? He was good. I just didn't have my long-view glasses on, but God did. Ron's losing his eye to cancer is what has brought about a forty-year ministry of writing songs for children, a ministy that we would have had no other way.

When Ron and I prayed for our son's healing from 1998 until 2013, was God not good because he answered our prayers differently than we wanted? He was and continues to be good.

Trials bring me closer to God because when I "live by faith" I have to humble myself to His will. When my will is broken and I accept His as better, my heart softens. If and when I harden my heart, it only destroys my relationship with my all-powerful, omnipotent, all-knowing Savior who created me and gifted me with salvation by His own tremendous sorrow, pain, and suffering on the cross. Trusting God in the hard times is when He is most glorified.

Since our Jonathan first became ill twenty-plus years ago, I have heard stories from many of you of a similar type. It takes a kind of courage to rise to the demands of mental illness in your life or in the life of your loved one. Courage comes in different guises in each of our lives. It is always challenging to step out of a comfort zone and rise to a new difficult task presented us. The courage you display in your situation, however, helps give others endurance to keep on keeping on themselves.

Jonathan's story is not yet over.

When dealing with mental illness, you must become a rock of perseverance. Some of you are in the throes of seeking answers on how to navigate your newly found challenge. Some of you have already discovered the God-given physical, emotional, and spiritual strength needed to rise to the assignment. The journey is very fluid. Wherever you are on yours, steadfastly moving in the right direction of faith is the only course to survival and success. No matter the pain, and sometimes because of the pain, we come out stronger than when we went in. We may not see at the time, but upon reflection.

When God allows difficulty in our lives, we need each other. The support we receive somehow helps as we share our sorrows, joys, and victories. Especially helpful is having someone come along side who has felt the same pain. We can be assured that Jesus always understands because of the sorrows He took on the cross just for us. Two are better than one— Jesus and you.

Like skydiving, once you jump into your new challenge, you are in flight. You aren't exactly certain where you will land, but you are not going back. But God. *But God. But God* is often my cry. I can never doubt. If I do, the Devil wins. I cannot and must not be a defeated Christian. But God. Everything depends on Him: His vision for our lives, His understanding of the human nature He gives us, and His sustaining energy.

As you climb your mountain, your life-lifting determination will be exhilarating. You will face your fear with style and a smile. When you are the caregiver, you become an example of a trainer, cheerleader, and coach. When you are the one dealing with illness, you become an example of how to recognize and accept the prognosis, enduring despite pain. *Acceptance with contentment* trumps *anger with bitterness* every time. With God's help, we can be the victor. The acceptance train will be gliding down the track, and we will be on it!

The best caregiver and caree inspire through and despite difficulty. You do this through your challenges, using imagination and creativity in dealing with them. Your supporters may sometimes be few, temperaments unpredictable, and succeeding uncertain, but press on. Your confidence will be displayed at all cost. Step by step, day by day, your lemons become lemonade.

Through your focusing on the job at hand, you gain endurance and end up guiding the people entrusted to you along a path. You are making it a path of courage and determination. Unexpectedly, before you know what is happening, you and those around you will realize you are a part of something bigger than yourselves—God's amazing plan! You are exhibiting a kind of courage.

The reward of accomplishing the assignments God has given us is enough. The courage you are displaying is investing into the lives of other people. People are the only investment we will take to heaven with us. What higher calling can equal that?

The year 2020 will always be remembered as a time of challenges: political uncertainty, economic instability, and fear of sickness. So much upheaval has happened with riots, looting, burning of businesses, and defunding of the police—all causing us to be shaken to the core. We are in a worldly warfare. Satan wants to defeat us and make us useless for God instead of useful.

We as Christians have such a higher calling than just existing for the here and now. We are made for more than just making it through this year and then the next. We are here not to build our own kingdom but to build the Kingdom of God.

I heard a preacher say that our eternal life is not in the future but begins the moment we accept Christ as Savior. If this be true, those of us who are God's children have already begun our journey into eternal life. Death on earth just transitions us into our future in heaven. Praise God, our citizenship is so much greater than what we have now. We are not for this world—hallelujah!

I would like to share a few subsidiary reasons why I wrote this book:

1. **Mental illness is not often talked about.** It is stigmatized. When you or a loved one live with mental illness, you are afraid

to talk about it, even afraid to get help. Many times you get little to no support, even though this illness can be one of the most devastating in existence.

2. **Mental illness is not understood.** I want you to get a glimpse into what someone goes through who lives with mental illness. Mental illness is as individual as the individuals that have it. But there are common threads through them all. Of course, some are more serious like Jonathan's.

3. **Mental illness is often not counseled effectively and appropriately.** I want Christians to know better how to counsel someone with mental illness. I want to warn caregivers, counselors, and family members of the serious consequences of this disease and the importance of seeking medical attention when the circumstances demand. I want to combat the often hurtful and damaging idea that it is merely a spiritual issue that can be "cured" if the sufferer becomes more spiritually minded. In my opinion, if this were the case, everyone who is not a Christian would have some type of a mental disorder. Someone with mental illness most likely feels guilty that he is sick because of something he has done. The last thing that should be added to his guilt is that it is his fault he is sick.

There are people all around you who live with some form of mental illness. I want to reiterate that one out of five people are likely affected, therefore, its members are everywhere. Grace is essential when speaking with others regarding mental illness. The possibility exists that they live with it or have a loved one or friend who does. There should be no stigma for any illness—only compassion, respect, and heartfelt sympathy.

Actually, many sufferers are in denial because they don't want the label of "mental illness." Taking a psychopathic medicine, in their view, is essentially admitting they are weak. Thus, the stigma lives on, if only in our minds.

Our beloved firstborn Jonathan developed clinical depression/schizophrenia when he was only eighteen years old. Yes, I would change Jonathan's story if I could. I would rewrite it with health and success and a glorious happy ending. It would be a much longer story with valiant and noble spiritual triumph, with a wife and children filled with laughter and normality, free of tragedy and that awful villain, mental illness. What I would not change is God's design, God's purpose, God's plan, and God's will. Nor would I want to change the valuable lessons our entire family has learned through the journey.

Jonathan was conceived during the time of Ron's cancer adversity, lived a life in spite of adversity, trusted God through adversity, and finally took his life because of adversity. One thing is for sure, there is adversity no more for Jonathan, only glory!

I am grateful to God for giving our family the gift of Jonathan. I would not trade that gift for the world, even though for only thirty-four years. Some only get to enjoy their children for thirty-four days or thirty-four months. I am grateful for the time we had. God gave us Jonathan for a purpose—for us to enjoy him and for him to enjoy us.

We don't get to choose what trials we will go through or how long they will last. God is creating a colorful tapestry out of our life, made from all kinds of fabrics and shapes. The backside view of the tapestry looks messy, gnarled, ugly, with no artistry or design, and makes no sense. God, however, can see both sides at once. When we get to our eternal home, however, I believe we will view the tapestry head on, in all its beauty—the one God was creating all along.

> *He hath made every thing beautiful in his time: also he hath set the world in their heart, so that no man can find out the work that God maketh from the beginning to the end. (Ecclesiastes 3:11)*

God knew before He created Jon that he would reside on this earth for a brief time. Jonathan fought spiritual battles, but as well brought glory to God during his short life. His legacy of trusting and loving God lives on through the beautiful music he wrote.

*I know that, whatsoever God doeth, it shall be for ever: nothing
can be put to it, nor any thing taken from it. (Ecclesiastes 3:14)*

Jonathan's sacred melodies he wrote have made the texts soar in hearts
that would have otherwise been immune to the pain of their origin. His
illness brought a depth to our ministry. Our entire family has become
less judgmental and more empathetic to other's journeys of faith.

If Jonathan had not died, very few would be aware of his suffering.
Because of his suffering, many have opened their hearts to the gospel,
which was the greatest desire of Jon's life. Not in the way Ron and I
would have wished it, but we have been given a more expansive ministry
of helping the hurting.

Jonathan told me before he became ill that he would love to be a music
leader in a large church someday with an expansive music program. I
am guessing God is fulfilling his wish right now in a bigger way than
Jon could have ever dreamed possible.

The last melody Jonathan wrote before he died was the tune to "You
Are Always Good." The message of God's goodness through trials is so
important. The thought overwhelms me and becomes the fuel by which
I keep going. I try numerous times to write lyrics for the thoughts of
God's goodness that I have in my heart, but without success. I have to
face it; I do not possess the gift of lyric writing.

I give my ideas and Jon's melody to our friend, Chris Anderson, who
is a very brilliant lyric writer. Chris pens a beautiful verse to Jonathan's
haunting melody. Chris says he writes these lyrics as Jonathan's testimony,
just as "Rejoice in the Lord" is Ron's. I feel that the resulting melody and
verse is literally a match made in heaven.

I love Jon's beautiful smile!

Dear Jesus, thank you again for the gift of Jonathan.
Thank you for giving him life.
He made our lives better . . .
Thank you for giving him the gift of music.
Thank you for loving him.
I am so grateful Jonathan loved You.
Thank you for placing him in our family.
I will celebrate his life because: God is always, only good.

You Are Always Good
Lyrics: Chris Anderson; Music: Jonathan Hamilton
© 2014 by Majesty Music, Inc.

Looking back, I can see Your fingerprints upon my life
always seeking my best.
There were times when Your way would make no sense;
but as You said, You have never left.

Refrain
You are always good; You are only good;
You are always good to me.
Though my eyes can't see, help my heart believe
You are always only good.

Looking in, I can see my frailty;
my sin is great, and my strength is so small.
Still You stay, and Your mercy shelters me;
You hold my hand, and You hear my call.

Looking up, I can see Your sympathy;
I doubt myself, but I'm sure of Your love.
Lavish grace was poured out at Calvary,
securing me for our home above.

You Are Always Good

CHLOE

Chris Anderson

Jonathan Hamilton

1. Look - ing back, I can see Your fin - ger-prints up - on my life al - ways
2. Look - ing in, I can see my frail - ty; my sin is great, and my
3. Look - ing up, I can see Your sym - pa - thy; I doubt my - self, but I'm

seek - ing my best. There were times when Your way would make no sense; but
strength is so small. Still You stay, and Your mer - cy shel - ters me; You
sure of Your love. Lav - ish grace was poured out at Cal - va - ry, se -

as You said, You have nev - er left.
hold my hand, and You hear my call.
cur - ing me for our home a - bove.

Refrain

You are al - ways good; You are on - ly good; You are al - ways good to me. Though my

eyes can't see, help my heart be - lieve You are al - ways on - ly good.